A REAL-LIFE GUIDE TO ORGANIZATIONAL CHANGE

❖

A REAL-LIFE GUIDE TO ORGANIZATIONAL CHANGE

❖

George Blair and Sandy Meadows

Gower

© George Blair and Sandy Meadows 1996

Published by
Gower Publishing Limited
Gower House
Croft Road
Aldershot
Hampshire GU11 3HR
England

Gower
Old Post Road
Brookfield
Vermont 05036
USA

British Library Cataloguing in Publication Data
Blair, George
A real-life guide to organizational change
1. Re-engineering (Management) 2. Organizational change
I. Title II. Meadows, Sandy
658.4'063

ISBN 0 566 07711 6

Library of Congress Cataloging-in-Publication Data
Blair, George, 1949–
A real-life guide to organizational change/George Blair and Sandy Meadows.
p. cm.
Includes index.
ISBN 0—566–07711–6
1. Organizational change. I. Meadows, Sandy, 1952–
HD58.8.B549 1996
658.4'08—dc20   96–8723
                                                CIP

Typeset in Great Britain

Britain by

CONTENTS

FIGURES

TABLES

PREFACE

Do you return from management courses inspired by exciting new visions but wondering how to make them happen?

Do you read reviews of the ideas of the latest management guru but question whether they will ever work in your organization?

Do you have an impressive library of management books, but are unsure what to do with them?

Do you wonder why the next guru contradicts the one who went before?

Are you puzzled as to why the rising star organizations favoured by gurus decline after a few years?

If the answer to any of these questions is yes, then this book is for you.

This is a voyage of discovery for busy managers who see that survival in the stormy seas of change involves more than holding on to the wreckage. Unlike their slowly drowning colleagues, they are not seduced by the temporary sense of security to be had by clinging on to what is known and loved. They can see the island and have the vision of how to get there. What are their chances of success? This book is for confident captains of *Titanics*, powering through the waves, moving ever-closer to the unseen icebergs. It is also for those in coves, sheltering from storms, who do not realize that they are drifting towards the rocks. We should not forget the highly competent cross-channel ferry captain whose aspiration is to be at the helm of a transatlantic liner and who wants help in making this transition.

We have selected the best from the international menu of management and organizational approaches to change. We will help you select your main course to suit your organizational taste. We advise you on the combination of dishes that will enhance or detract from your choice. There are health warnings on some potentially fatal combinations. All selections must be made in the full knowledge of the current reality in your organization. This practical approach is supported by diagnostic tools to find out the current state of your organization to help you choose from the many checklists for action.

As in the best restaurants, the menu may change with fashion, but the new dishes use the same ingredients. Similarly management ideas may change with fashion, but the underlying concepts do not lose their validity. We offer you prepared food for thought for your organizational microwave, rather than exotic dishes that are difficult to copy.

THE WAY FORWARD

To ensure that you do not consume any of the courses in the wrong order, or even miss them, we have provided the following main menu. It highlights the decisions that need to be made and their logical consequences. This ensures that you can pursue consistent strategies. The book is divided into four main parts. At the end of each part you will have designed the menu for your own organization. You can view these steps as four separate courses. Each is distinct but as with any meal their interdependencies must be taken into consideration. A decision on each needs to be taken before you move on to the next step. The first course is the starter. This requires an analysis of the reality in your own organization – where are you starting from? This is followed by a look into the future – where do you want to go and how will you take your organization with you? The main course, which can often result in much indigestion, asks – what approaches will you adopt to get there? The final course ensures that everything within the organization supports the required change. You therefore need to determine what supporting strategies you will use to underpin your approach.

Bon appétit!

The authors would be pleased to talk through with you how you are bringing about organizational change and how you get on. Who knows, your work could appear as a case study in a future edition! You may contact us at:

Quadra Consulting
Mary Sheridan House
St. Thomas' Street
London
SE1 9RS

Telephone: 0171–955 8851/2
Fax: 0171–955 4856

George Blair
Sandy Meadows

ACKNOWLEDGEMENTS

We would particularly like to thank Stephen Connock, Philip Gill, Perry Walker, John Armour, Tony Margree and Dr Gordon Pearson for their constructive criticism and support. We must also acknowledge the contribution of information and ideas from the countless authors on this fascinating and evolving subject that we read whilst researching this book. Last, but definitely not least, a big thank you to our 'partners' in both the personal and business sense Brenda Allan, Bob Meadows, Peter Rankin and Wayne Rees.

GB
SM

PART I

STARTING POINT

Chaos often breeds life, when order breeds habit.
Henry Adams, 1907

1
WHERE ARE YOU NOW?

Even victors are by victory undone
John Dryden

WHY NO COMPANY IS SAFE

Organizational change is no longer the optional extra it used to be when it was undertaken only by ponderous, overweight organizations. Then organizations considered it only when they were in danger of being overtaken by their fitter, more youthful competitors. More recently it has been undertaken by the leaders of the pack who, no longer content to be first, want to break the record in every race they enter. Now even organizations in the main bunch are seeking to improve their performance by reorganizing.

Change of all kinds – economical, social, cultural, technological and political – is occurring at accelerating rates. In the past, change in both business and the wider society was incremental. Now it can, and probably is, happening to all individuals and organizations. Not to change means certain death – the only question is when. Even highly successful organizations need to change as their time in the sun is ever-shortening. Too many of them are like the unicorn – they don't plan their route to the ark until the flood is upon them. They try to squeeze ever-diminishing profits from products that are increasingly outdated. The hardest change to contemplate is to scale down or even abandon successful activities. Yet this is the very time when an organization has the powerful springboard of success, with the money, the staff morale and corporate confidence to explore the new. Companies facing difficulties have even less time to delay.

Huge, multinationals have been humbled by more agile, market oriented competitors. General Motors is a case in point. Once it dominated the US car market to such an extent that there was talk of using anti-trust laws to break its hold. Now Japanese competition has achieved this instead. In 1991, its North American operations lost up to $8 billion and there are plans to close 21 factories with a loss of 74 000 jobs. What are the factors behind such threats to well-established companies? Many of the 'excellent' companies praised by Peters and Waterman (*In Search of Excellence*, 1982) have gone into decline. Indeed, between 1956 and 1992 71 American companies have slipped off Fortune's list of the top 100 companies (*The Economist*, 4 April 1992, p.15). Interestingly, Japanese companies have had their casualties as well. Two-thirds of companies lose their top 100 listing every 30 years (*The Economist*, 4 April 1992, p.20).

Another significant change is that products and services have much shorter lives, which places a premium on being able to develop and produce new products and services as quickly as possible. Being first to the market results in high profit margins, before competitors catch up, and a longer product life in which to earn further profits. Therefore, big, inflexible organizations and those with poorly coordinated design and production functions are very vulnerable. They are like juggernauts caught in slow moving traffic that are overtaken by faster, more manoeuvrable motorbikes. In addition, with much shorter product lives, selling in volume to world markets is essential for many producers. It is only through worldwide sales that they can achieve a large enough volume of sales to obtain a good return.

Competition has increased greatly both from well-established economies such as Japan and from newly industrialized countries on the Pacific Rim. Taiwan, for instance, is taking over work from British Aerospace. The productivity of China and South Korea has doubled in the last ten years (Royal Society of Arts, 1994, p.4). It is sobering to think that industrial giants such as Sony and Honda date only from the post-war era. Political changes such as the collapse of communism in Eastern Europe may lead to more lower cost competition.

Other factors leading to the globalization of production are falling trade barriers and low transport costs by sea and air. Transnational corporations find it much easier to coordinate their activities through vastly improved tele-communication networks.

Britain performs poorly in terms of international competitiveness. It fell four places to 18th in a ranking covering a wide range of indices compiled by the World Economic Forum of Switzerland (*Guardian*, 6 September 1995, p.3). The way is led by the USA, Singapore, Hong Kong, Japan, Switzerland and Germany. Our highly rated service sector (4th) compared with a dismal manufacturing base that was ranked 35th out of 48. Only 6 per cent of UK companies were considered world class in a recent survey (RSA, 1994, p.9). We score badly on education, the motivation of our workforce, equal opportunities and on crime. The bright spots are inward investment, freedom of action for foreign investors and our financial markets.

The service sector has felt itself protected from global competition. This confidence can be misplaced as countries such as the Philippines and Mauritius do some of the paper work for European countries. Data can be transmitted from Europe at the end of the day to be entered into a computer database available for worldwide access the next day. European organizations with highly skilled staff are under threat as well. An Indian company won the contract to write software for the London Underground by heavily undercutting the prices charged by its European-based competition. Due to time differences, the Indian day shift can replace the British night shift, thus speeding up collaborative work with the intercontinental teams bridging day and night. British companies act as agents for some Indian software houses. Indian computer companies have several strengths: they benefit from good education and English is widely spoken. India can attract its brightest and most ambitious people to computing as it is seen as a very high status occupation. Some of their key personnel are former computer science graduates who used to work on software for NASA.

Customers want more choice. Many manufacturers have been forced to move away from long production runs of a few products to short runs of a wider range of products, in direct response to customer orders. Flexibility and close cooperation on the shop floor have become vital.

Customers are more demanding and quality conscious: what they found acceptable five years ago, they now regard as substandard. Leading organizations now aim to 'delight' customers by exceeding their expectations. Merely satisfying customers is seen as belonging to the 1980s. Loyal customers are heavy spenders and make a disproportionately large contribution to profits. Companies that lose customers have to spend increasing amounts on advertising in the hope of attracting new interest. Those that can no longer compete on quality are forced to compete on price, leading to lower profit margins and often a fall in total profits. Poor standards are often linked to dissatisfied staff who are under pressure to cut corners to reduce costs.

The Japanese are dedicated to systematically reducing costs by eliminating waste. They define waste in broad terms to include anything that does not add value, such as overheads or indirect costs that cannot be fully justified. They reduced levels of stocks and replaced inefficient production systems many years ago in their search for zero defects. They regard as value only what customers are willing to pay for, which excludes the added cost of waste. Their emphasis is on working smarter rather than merely harder.

Technological change can make products and processes obsolete. For example, will a recent development such as the growth of video shops be swept away by the latest communication systems? Without having to leave home, viewers will be able to dial the video of their choice, which will be sent electronically to their television. Insurance companies with expensive networks of agents are being undercut by competitors using telephone-based services instead. The support from a sophisticated computer programme enables one member of staff to give a quotation and complete the sale over the telephone.

Corporate knowledge is not enough, however. Exciting discoveries need real commitment to see them through. Xerox virtually invented the personal computer yet it never exploited its great achievement. This often happens because organizations are unwilling to take risks. The risk not only of possibly losing money, but of the dislocation of substantial change.

Rapid change is placing a premium on knowledge workers and knowledge intensive industries, which in turn requires a continuous investment in training and development. Yet, only 25 per cent of the UK workforce has intermediate qualification compared with 63 per cent in Germany (Department of Trade and Industry, 1993, p.217).

UK and American companies often fail to meet the challenges of customer orientation, continuous quality improvement, and sustained investment in training development and technology because of their obsession with short-term profits. The interests of shareholders and the avoidance of take-overs dominate the thinking of senior management. This can result in indifferent performance from staff who feel undervalued. They are also likely to resist change as they are unlikely to be involved or adequately rewarded for the inevitable upheaval. Customers and quality can also be sacrificed on the altar of short-term profitability.

Many organizations still treat suppliers in a cavalier way, chopping and changing them regularly for short-term price advantage. The Japanese have been much more successful in reducing costs over a longer period of time by developing more supportive relationships. Their suppliers who enjoy greater security invest more heavily in designing and developing components that are better suited to their customers' needs.

Organizations need to be socially and environmentally sensitive if they are to avoid the attention of effective and articulate pressure groups and perhaps worse. At the height of the Brixton riots in the 1980s, the local Marks and Spencer store survived unscathed. Its escape was not due to a love of its products, it was due to its success in recruiting a significant number of staff from the local black community. Organizations that will thrive in the future will relate closely and consistently to all their stakeholders, be they shareholders, customers, employees, suppliers or the wider community. Many companies have ignored such threats to their cost.

Size and power may lead to a dangerous overconfidence – the 'Titanic syndrome'. The proud boast of the liner's owners was that it was unsinkable. To their cost, they grossly underestimated the risk from icebergs, and when the unthinkable happened, they were unprepared: there were too few lifeboats so most passengers drowned. The computer industry provides an interesting example of how that sudden sinking feeling can affect an industrial giant, as the case study opposite shows.

The very reason for a company's success can become a source of its future weakness. It may be unwilling to abandon activities that remain profitable in the short to medium term, yet stand in the way of its future developments. On the other hand, its competitors may well be faster moving as they are not weighed down by such legacies. A similar problem is that organizations can persist with tried and tested approaches with which they feel very comfortable, long after they are of value. These neurotic organizations, like their human counterparts, are locked into redundant behaviour. Their response to new problems is to do more of the same. Companies can even ignore their own revolutionary discoveries because they fear such change would upset their smooth running bureaucratic machines. The Palo Alto Research Center invested heavily in new developments and gave its researchers considerable freedom. It practically invented the microcomputer but did not develop it commercially.

WHAT IS YOUR CURRENT POSITION?

Until the 1980s the primary purpose of managers was fairly clear. They were

Case study: A humbled giant – Digital

Digital had acquired a culture where responsibility was evaded at all costs. It had large overheads, extensive manufacturing capacity and a bloated sales force. It made losses in the four years up to 1994 and its share price fell from $110 to $15 over the same period. Digital was undercut by smaller, faster-moving organizations that bought in more of their components. It responded by cutting 20 000 jobs and drastically reducing factory and office space.

The core of its problem was holding on to what had made it great. Digital was living in the past in the era of large, highly profitable computers. It had a dominant culture of engineering that was increasingly out of touch with customers. Computing had become a mass market whilst Digital concentrated on specialist sectors. It was also unfocused and tried to make too many components in-house. It had abandoned a successful network of dealers in order to increase its profit margin on each sale and gain greater control.

The company has now rebuilt its network of dealers and has adopted the mass marketing strategy of its competitors. It is aiming to reduce its administrative costs to 22 per cent of revenues and bring research and development costs down to 12 per cent.

Source: Summarized from *The Financial Times*, 26 July 1994

there to set up work practices and procedures and to manage day-to-day operations efficiently and effectively. They were judged on their ability to repeat the same process to the same standard within a stable environment. The managers provided the brainpower and the workers provided the hands. Loyalty was the order of the day in exchange for which organizations adopted a paternalistic approach to both managers and staff. Long, reliable service was rewarded by progress up the hierarchy. This was accompanied by tangible status symbols such as a carpeted office, a reserved parking space and a separate dining room.

Times have changed. Managers still have to deliver products and services in the quantity and quality required but nowadays they are also being called on to orchestrate significant organizational change. Tom Peters draws attention to this in his book *Thriving on Chaos* (Peters 1989)

> Most fundamentally, the times demand that the flexibility and love of change replace our long-standing penchant for mass production and mass market, based as it is upon a relatively predictable set of circumstances that have vanished.

Organizations are increasingly finding themselves with structures that inhibit, rather than facilitate change and flexibility. They have difficulty in coming to terms with change and how to learn to balance continuity and discontinuity. A further problem is that casualties cannot be put to one side while managers plan and implement the necessary changes.

The task is a very complex one. McKinsey's seven-point plan illustrates that structure, strategy, style, shared values, systems, skills and staff are all interconnected so it is rarely possible to change one element in the mix without affecting the rest. The trouble is that many of the cross impacts cannot be anticipated (see Chapter 2 for more on the seven-point plan).

A further difficulty is the ambiguity, uncertainty, and emotion that pervades every aspect of the change process. Most people find change threatening because it involves the unknown: it means acquiring new skills; it means altering the familiar 'safe' status quo; it may undermine power bases and generally involves a new order.

Before we can decide on how best to meet these challenges, we need to understand our current position. Identify for your own organization the following factors:

○   External threats
○   The type of structure
○   Where it is in its life cycle
○   Its overall health

This will help you decide which menu of change is best suited to your organization.

EXTERNAL THREATS

Score your own company against the risk factors listed in Table 1.1. High scores in any of these factors indicate that perhaps you are not as safe as you thought you were. High scores in all of them suggest you need to inflate the dinghy! For example, low scores in factors 1 to 3 would suggest that you have processes that support speedy development from design to production, flexible production techniques and quality. Therefore, you can respond better to threats from risk factors 5 and 6. On the other hand, you may be in an unstable environment. High scores in factors 1 to 3 suggest that your processes are out of step with existing needs and coupled with high risks in factors 5 and 6 would be fatal. Beware of factor 4, the unpredictable wild card, as it can hit even the best prepared organization. Technology can make your products or your processes obsolete overnight.

ORGANIZATIONAL STRUCTURES AND THEIR IMPACT

Structures can have a big impact on an organization's capacity to change and how sharply aware it is of the outside world of customers and competitors. Some organizations are introverted. They are inward looking and focus on themselves without glancing over their shoulders at the competition. Horizon scanners, on the other hand are organizations which are highly receptive to ideas and innovations that can be adapted to improve their performance. They continually

TABLE 1.1   RISK FACTORS

Risk factor	Level of risk				
	Very low 1	Low 2	Average 3	High 4	Very high 5
1. More demanding and sophisticated customers					
2. Demand for ever-expanding product range					
3. Shorter life cycle of products and services					
4. Technological obsolescence					
5. New, more flexible entrants into market					
6. Global competition					
Total					

scan the activities of their competitors and any other organizations from which they might learn. Such organizations can also be centralized or decentralized.

In centralized organizations the top managers make all the important decisions. Consequently, there is a lack of delegation. Typically, there are many tiers of management and roles are rigidly defined. In the past, the centralized organization was the preferred model as it could achieve economies of scale. It could have an introvert focus and yet survive, as for many competition was less intense. Another advantage of centralized organizations is that decisions are usually consistent and different parts of the organization are unlikely to have to compete against each other in the same market-place. However, decisions can take longer to make because of the extended lines of communication and the many facets of the organization that may have to be considered, making the company vulnerable to more agile competitors in an era of rapid change.

Decentralized organizations devolve as much responsibility as possible to the lower levels. Top managers set and monitor a few, very important measures by which they judge performance. There tend to be fewer tiers of management. Roles and procedures may be less well defined and easy to change. Academic institutions and advertising and public relations agencies may have many of these features. The advantages and disadvantages of this type of organization are the converse of centralized organizations.

The different types of organizations can be charted using introvert–extrovert and centralized – decentralized scales. The examples in Figure 1.1 show general tendencies and therefore should not be taken too literally, for no two organizations are identical. The figure shows that banks are centralized and universities are decentralized, yet they both have tended to be introvert organizations. Car manufacturers and advertising agencies tend to be extrovert organizations while advertising agencies can be more decentralized decision makers. With the growth of competition throughout all these sectors, these differences are becoing less extreme.

If you are a *centralized introvert* you are vulnerable to all the risk factors highlighted in Table 1.1. On the other hand, if you are a *decentralized introvert* you are likely to have the capability to respond more quickly to change, but because you are not routinely scanning the horizon you may not anticipate the threats until it is too late. Introvert tendencies can become very deep rooted when organizations rely mainly on internal promotion. The outside world and the ways of others can seem alien and unwelcome. This was the position of Woolworth until new blood from outside retailing led to significant improvements in the 1980s.

If you are a *centralized extrovert* you will see the threats but find it difficult to respond quickly. On the other hand, the *decentralized extrovert* organization

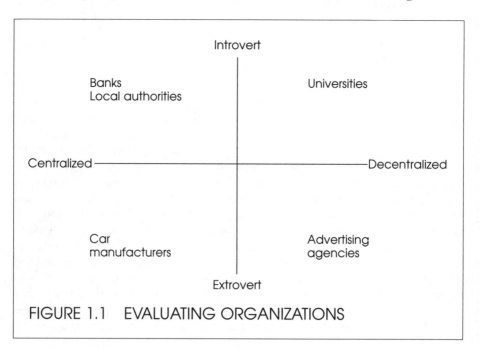

FIGURE 1.1   EVALUATING ORGANIZATIONS

is alert to its customers and competition, will see the threats and is flexible enough to turn them into opportunities.

Using Figure 1.2 locate the current position of your own organization, and the place where you would ideally like it to be. How far and in which direction has it got to move?

THE ORGANIZATIONAL LIFE CYCLE

Companies, like products, are subject to a life cycle. As infants they tend to start as small, entrepreneurial organizations. Their extrovert gaze keeps them close to their customers. Communications are quick and direct as there are usually few levels of management.

In maturity, the growth in sales leads to a further expansion of staff. Roles often become more specialized and fragmented. Top management adds layers of managers as it wants to retain control. The voice of the customer is more distant and harder to hear. Ageing companies may grow even larger and acquire a prestigious head office. Regional offices are opened adding more levels of management. Research and development moves further away from production. Organizational politics absorbs more time than external focus. Customers do not have priority in these introverted organizations. If they fail to diversify, organizations become very vulnerable to the life cycle of their products. Because of their past success, 'Titanic' over-confidence sets in. At this point organizations become vulnerable to more agile competitors. The marble from the head office foyer could be recycled for the organization's tombstone.

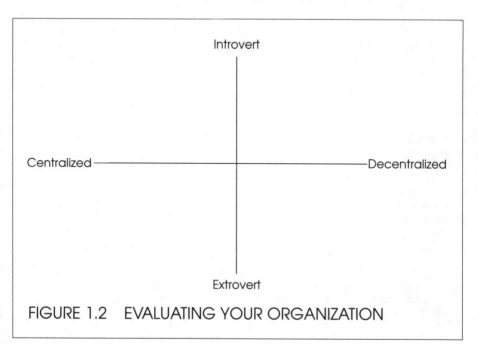

FIGURE 1.2   EVALUATING YOUR ORGANIZATION

It is very difficult for a mature organization to grow and age without becoming unhealthy. It is more common to find mature organizations slipping into the centralized introvert category with all the accompanying risks.

Where do you think your company is in its life cycle? Using the matrix in Table 1.2, which is based on Pedler, Burgoyne and Boydell's book *The Learning Company* (1991), score your own organization.

Where does your organization fit most closely on the matrix? Ensure that you

TABLE 1.2   YOUR ORGANIZATION'S STAGE IN THE COMPANY LIFE CYCLE

Factors	Type of company						
	Infant	Pioneer	Rational	Established	Wilderness	Dying	Transforming
Is your company still owned and run by the original founders?	Yes	Yes	Unlikely	No	No	No	New owners, may be management buy out
Are most staff engaged on direct customer contact activities	Yes	Yes	50/50	No	No	No	Yes, moving back to that direction
Do you have more than three tiers of management?	No	No	Yes	Yes	Yes	Yes	In the middle of delayering
Do you have well-defined operating procedures and processes?	No	No	Yes	Yes	Yes	Yes	Flexibility is being re-introduced and processes are being reviewed
Are your support functions, e.g. personnel, a head office function?	No	No	Most are	Yes	Yes	Yes	These functions are now being devolved
Are most important decisions made by top management alone?	No	No	Yes	Yes	Yes	Yes	Decision making is becoming participative and devolved
Is the market share for your products fairly stable?	No	No	We think so	We think so	We don't know, it is too frag-mented	Shrink-ing	No

use this matrix to develop a biography for your own company so that you know where it is in its life cycle and therefore the inherent difficulties it will face. For example, infant and pioneering companies are likely to be more open to change in general; dying and transforming companies may accept change as a necessary evil; rational and established companies may be too complacent and self-satisfied to accept its inevitability. Unfortunately, wilderness companies may be just too introvert and may have lost touch completely with the reality of the pace of change. Change is still possible in all the stages but obviously the approach used must be carefully tailored in the light of the stage your organization has reached.

UNHEALTHY ORGANIZATIONS

Unhealthy organizations are often the first to suffer when survival depends on being able to change constantly. No organization is perfect but centralized introvert organizations have more unhealthy characteristics than others. To survive, organizations must attack the unhealthy signs, such as those listed below:

1. Organizational structure
    O The power structure dictates what is permissible behaviour.
    O Managers talk about pushing power down but there is no real empowerment or delegation.
    O Several layers of jobs exist simply to ensure that no one makes mistakes.
    O The purpose of the organization is vague.
    O Roles and responsibilities are unclear and overlap.
    O People in one part of the organization have no idea what the other parts do.
    O Internal, inter-functional conflicts escalate.
2. Job design and processes
    O People are preoccupied with policies, procedures, rules and precedent.
    O There is an abundance of paperwork.
    O Meetings are endless and follow up is non-existent.
3. Management attitudes
    O Managers are reluctant to develop their staff for fear of creating rivals.
    O Senior managers have permanent long-term contracts as opposed to rolling renewable ones.
    O Discussion means waiting for the boss to say what is right.
    O New ideas and talent are suppressed by a management that feels it must be the source of all that is creative and praiseworthy.
    O Key decisions are taken without any consultation with those affected, or any concern over their anxieties.
4. Motivation and involvement of staff

O   Induction is seen as an event and not a process.
O   Staff feel undervalued.
O   The workforce is littered with the casualties of previous quick fix solutions.
O   Rumours abound.
O   Resignations take management by surprise.
O   Recruiters take on staff in their image.

5.   Reward strategy
O   Key objectives are either not identified or no action is taken when they are not achieved.
O   The appraisal system has no significant impact on performance.
O   Employees get little or no feedback on their performance.
O   Compensation does not reflect what people really do.
O   The promotion system does not reward individual merit.

Do you recognize any of these signs? You can score your organization against these dimensions using Table 1.4 in tools for management action at the end of this chapter.

HOW HEALTHY IS YOUR ORGANIZATION?

Table 1.3 has been used to rate the health of three organizations. Table 1.4 gives you the chance to rate your own organization. It can make for a fascinating comparison. Ensure that you get the perspectives from staff in different parts of the organization. This will show whether you are all starting from a shared view or whether there needs to be some discussion to draw your views closer together. Get your friends in other companies to complete the exercise too.

TABLE 1.3   ORGANIZATIONAL HEALTH – HOW SOME ORGANIZATIONS SCORE

Factor	Score			
	Very poor 1	Poor 2	Good 3	Very good 4
1. Closeness to customers		Ch CS	NHS	
2. Willingness to act	CS	Ch NHS		
3. Entrepreneurial style and tolerance of failure	Ch CS	NHS		
4. Productivity through people		Ch CS	NHS	
5. Autonomy: level of delegation	Ch	CS	NHS	
6. Communication of information	Ch	CS NHS		
7. Bottom up versus top down planning		Ch CS NHS		
8. Visibility of top management	CS	Ch	NHS	
9. Tiers of management	Ch	CS	NHS	
10. Movement and cooperation between functions		Ch	NHS	CS
11. Range of businesses	CS		Ch	NHS

Organization	Score
Ch: a large UK charity	17
CS: a Civil Service department	19
NHS: a Trust Hospital	31

TABLE 1.4   HOW HEALTHY IS YOUR ORGANIZATION?

Factor	Score			
	Very poor 1	Poor 2	Good 3	Very good 4
1. Closeness to customers	Little interest in customers	Some response to customer needs	Often meet customer needs	Dedicated to meeting customer needs
2. Willingness to act	'Do nothing' the preferred option	Slight preference for action over inaction	Significant preference for action over inaction	Action based approach
3. Entrepreneurial style and tolerance of failure	None; failure avoidance endemic	Some; failure avoidance widespread	Substantial; emphasis on success	Focus on success with little failure avoidance
4. Productivity through people	Staff not valued	Staff are valued to some extent	Staff are valued	Staff considered to be of great value
5. Autonomy: level of delegation	Very little scope to act independently	Some scope to act independently	Considerable individual discretion	Largely autonomous
6. Communication of information	Very little	Some	Considerable	Very considerable: no secrets
7. Bottom up versus top down planning	Only top down	Largely top down	Half top down and half bottom up	Mainly bottom up
8. Visibility of top management	Invisible	Remote	Approachable	Very visible and accessible
9. Tiers of management	9 or more	7 to 8	6	5 or fewer
10. Movement and cooperation between functions	Very rare	Rare	Frequent	Very frequent
11. Range of businesses	Very diverse	Diverse	Similar	Very similar
Total				

The following inferences can be drawn from your scores:

15 and under   – poor; you may have a real struggle on your hands
16–24   – considerable scope for improvement
25–34   – quite good, some potential for improvement
35–44   – very good; case study material for management textbook.

CHECKLIST FOR MANAGEMENT ACTION

1.   What is your organization's current position?
        O   Is it safe?
        O   Is it already facing difficulties?
        O   Do you have the resources in staff and money to explore the new?
2.   What external threats is it facing?
3.   What type of structure does it have?
4.   Where is its main focus – internal or external?
5.   Where is it in its life cycle?
6.   How is its overall health?

END OF STOCK TAKE

You are probably now suffering from organizational indigestion, but do not panic – the cure follows. We will guide you through the many options and pitfalls in the next chapter.

2

WINNING SUPPORT FOR CHANGE

There is nothing more difficult to handle, more doubtful
of success, and more dangerous to carry through than
initiating changes in a state's constitution. The innovator
makes enemies of all those who prospered under the
old order and only luke warm support is forthcoming
from those who would prosper under the new.

Machiavelli, *The Prince*

In a fight between you and the world, back the world.

Franz Kafka

TO CHANGE OR NOT TO CHANGE?

Now that you are only too aware that no organization is safe, what do you do next? Are you looking around for the next Cambridge diet hoping to slip painlessly into the corporate bikini after a couple of weeks? If you are, we hope you did not pay for this book yourself as we cannot help you. Change is threatening and risky. Whoever said there is no gain without pain was certainly right.

Between two-thirds and three-quarters of all change programmes fail to meet their objectives, according to recent research. Yet the reality is that while maintaining the status quo is undoubtedly the most comfortable approach in the short term, it is the highest risk strategy of all. There are many examples of organizations who were leading the race, became complacent and stayed still too long. Competitors were stimulated to greater effort so that they could overtake them. Avoiding change in today's world is terminal, the only question is when.

❖ **Health warning +**

Change is a substantial task that requires a huge investment in time and resources.

STRATEGY FOR CHANGE

Change cannot be rushed. It must be planned and performed with all the skill and involvement that is required for a famous orchestra to perform a leading symphony. It can be led by a principal conductor or project manager but in the same way that each musician must understand the role they must play, have the capability and skills to do this and feel that they have some say in the general interpretation, so change must be introduced with the same degree of sensitivity. Unfortunately, in some organizations management views change more like an army exercise where the chief of staff carry out all the intricate planning down to the last detail and the 'troops' are expected to follow orders to the letter. This approach will just not work in an organization no matter how charismatic the leader. Time must be taken to prepare all the leading stakeholders for change. Their views and anxieties must be explored; their skills and capabilities enhanced, if necessary; they must be clear about their new role and contribute to its evolution. If you cut corners at this stage the result may be that your organizational orchestra is so fragmented that the brass section is playing a waltz whilst the strings are playing a polka and the wind instruments are not playing at all.

Stakeholder resistance cannot be underestimated. It will take many different forms. Powerful stakeholders may choose to exercise negative power and attempt to prevent change from occurring, particularly if the change may result in the erosion of either their power base or some of the status symbols that they currently enjoy. Less powerful stakeholders may experience great stress and anxiety and this will affect their day-to-day effectiveness and seriously undermine their confidence in bringing about successful change.

THE ROLE OF TOP MANAGEMENT IN CHANGE

The role of management today is to create and maintain a high rate of change, something that is particularly difficult in the UK. We have a particular love of the old and apparent contempt for the new. Even today in Britain the word 'new' is not an automatic selling point, but could suggest that the product is not adequately tried and tested, that it is possibly a gimmick. By contrast, in Japan newness and novelty are constantly sought and applauded, and German organizations share some of this attitude towards continuous improvement and innovation. Change, like all aspects of management and leadership requires understanding and attention to the fears of the people who are affected by it. To give the proposed change a good chance of success it is necessary to understand how the forces supporting and opposing change align themselves. Here the concept of force field analysis can be useful. See the section later in this chapter.

One of the significant factors in bringing about change is dissatisfaction with the current state. As Sir John Harvey-Jones writes in his book *Making it Happen* (1988), 'The engine of change is dissatisfaction with the present and the brakes of change are fear of the unknown and fear of the future.' Change is easy when the organization is obviously threatened and survival depends on changing the way things are done, but where in successful organizations does the impetus for change come from? It must originate from the senior managers painting a picture of the potential threats to survival that are currently unrecognized. You can define these threats, their sources and the environment in which you operate by using the analytical tools described in Chapter 3. Once you have this understanding of the environment, not to change is no longer an option.

Does your organization suffer from mantra management? Are your senior managers and chief executive regular course attendees who pick up new ideas wholesale? In consequence there may be a credibility gap between their words and their totally unchanged actions and behaviour. This reinforces the business as usual factor. This preference for 'new speak' over action can generate endless debate and a multiplicity of working parties at a theoretical level whilst the real issues for change remain unresolved.

❖   **Health warning +**

Change is a learning process. You have to make the discoveries yourself. You can benefit from the experience of others, but you have to work through the ideas so that they fit your organization.

So where do you begin in your own organization? Successful change must be led and supported at all times from the top. Change should not merely be given star billing at board meetings, conferences and awaydays but should be the number one priority in all senior managers' objectives. Every strategy, decision and message coming from the senior team must be seen to reinforce and support the change initiative. This takes time and effort as staff soon see through empty gestures. A frequent source of failure is when responsibility for change is delegated too far down the organization where there is insufficient power to cope with the inevitable conflict of interest.

You need to create a vision that gives a clear sense of direction and signposts a route along which the organization can chart its progress. Most change initiatives fail because managers embark upon them without a clear idea of what they are trying to achieve and how they will actually deliver change. The result is that managers do more of the same by attempting to solve a problem by trying harder with failed strategies. This method is more comfortable that adopting new, unfamiliar approaches. As the saying goes, when you are in a hole, stop digging. Organizations have to experience much grief before they do something different.

ADDRESSING STAFF AND OTHER STAKEHOLDERS

The impact of change cannot be assumed to be the same on all individuals and groups either within the organization or outside it. People will be affected differently, according to their degree of involvement and their vested interests.

You therefore need to identify all such stakeholders. They could include the following:

○   Shareholders
○   Employees
○   Unions
○   Suppliers
○   Customers
○   The local community

In previously stable business environments the concept of change is alien to all stakeholders. Where people have been damaged by seeing their colleagues sacked and jobs cut seemingly arbitrarily, in the wake of badly managed change, the resistance to further change will be high.

The one stakeholder that received all the attention in the past was the shareholder. Consequently organizations concentrated on short-term profitability and focused on payment of dividend rather than investing in the long-term future. The knowledge base is becoming one of an organization's major assets so it is vital to engage the hearts and minds of the workforce not just their hands as in the past. A token shareholding given to staff to make their interests similar to those of shareholders will not suffice; they need to be involved in all significant decisions. 'The empires of the future are the empires of the mind' (Winston Churchill).

There cannot be enough communication in all directions, up, down and across the organization. Every medium must be employed to put the message across. One organization used a query box in which staff placed their questions anonymously. Management pinned the answers on a notice board within twenty-four hours. Where the facility of electronic mail exists, a weekly news bulletin can be sent to all staff. Open forums can be used to generate staff feedback but great caution must be used to ensure that the size, seniority and functional mix do not inhibit the honest expression of opinion. One way to guard against heroic assumptions of staff support is to carry out staff surveys every six months. Staff anonymity is protected by using an external organization to collect and analyse the information.

Staff will probably feel threatened even if you have an ambitious communications programme. They may well go through a cycle of responding to the threat of change by denying that it affects their section. They can then withdraw and offer passive resistance, which can be both corrosive and difficult to pinpoint. They may be sad about what they are giving up and suffer guilt for those who are likely to lose out. This in turn can lead to anger. The cycle can go on repeating itself. One way to cut through this cycle is to select the first change project which is likely to result in a quick win. A success will strengthen the resolve of the change agents at all levels and give the doubters more to think about. There is a danger, though, that those with most to lose will become informed rather than uninformed critics.

If the change is to be participative, then people need the skills of brainstorming, problem solving and teamworking. Organizations need to 'carry their wounded and shoot their stragglers'. Thus a substantial investment in retraining loyal staff with obsolete skills is required to underline the fact that the organization genuinely values its staff. On the other hand, the organization will want to reinforce the message that there will not be a future within it for those who seek to undermine the change and hold the organization back.

Staff involvement can be readily accommodated in successful organizations but what happens in those facing significant downsizing? Many argue that 'turkeys will not vote for an early Christmas' and the same must apply with staff facing redundancy. The evidence from Thorn EMI suggests that this is not necessarily the case.

Fears of job cuts can be lessened by offering a generous voluntary redundancy scheme. An analysis of the age of the workforce will show the number eligible for early retirement. Offering an attractive package of training and development to all staff will improve morale to compensate for some of the likely lost promotional opportunities for the survivors.

Staff cannot be considered as a homogeneous group in relation to their commitment and willingness to embrace change. Those at the top have the opportunity to achieve significant success in masterminding change particularly if they have share options linked directly to profitability. The worst price they are likely to pay for failure is a golden parachute. At best, staff at the bottom of the organization will benefit from increased job satisfaction through involvement and greater training and development opportunities. At worst they face redundancy

Case study: Combining commitment with redundancies – Thorn EMI

The Hayes, Middlesex factory of EMI Music employed some 700 people in the production of vinyl discs and cassette tapes. The growing switch by consumers from discs and tapes to CDs meant a rapid reduction in the size of the operation and a reduction in the workforce to 150.

As part of the reorganization the company introduced total quality management (TQM) and applied for British Standards Institution quality standard BS5750. A TQM training module together with completion certificates was made available to the whole workforce and 75 per cent of employees undertook the business analysis necessary to write the manuals for TQM and BS5750.

After completion of the redundancy programme the relationship between Thorn EMI and its former employees remains strong, owing to a number of compensating benefits:

O   Training certification plus business process analysis skills increased their employability.

O   The strong relationships established in teamworking meant that they could use their new found expertise as basis for future networking.

In conclusion, enhancing future employability was successful as there were benefits to both sides, some of which were unexpected.

Source: RSA (1994), *Tomorrow's Company*, p. 16

but, generally, long-serving staff will receive a package fought for on their behalf by their staff organizations. In stark contrast to these groups, the middle managers who must deliver the change are often those that stand to lose the most. They will have fewer opportunities for promotion and many will lose their jobs. The survivors' roles will be radically altered. They will no longer be able to supervise their staff closely as they will be responsible for many more staff. They will become coaches, facilitators and coordinators. Their status will be severely undermined by the loss of perks such as designated parking places, higher cc cars and their exclusive access to much of the organization's information will be lost. Middle managers represent a significant group potentially opposed to change and their commitment must be harnessed otherwise they will be preoccupied with preserving their own status.

The degree of staff involvement can vary between that traditionally found in the West and that found in the East. In the West, new visions and strategies are often drawn up quite quickly with little staff involvement. A great deal of time and effort is then spent trying to sell ideas to staff that do not own them. In the East the emphasis is the other way around. A basic decision for your organization at this point is which of these philosophies to adopt. This decision should take account of the reality of current staff involvement, including the willingness of senior managers to share the sensitive strategic and operational information that is fundamental to truly involving staff. Unfortunately, for the 'fudgers' there is no halfway house. Staff will sense immediately if what is described as staff involvement is, in reality, a staff suggestion scheme or ad hoc involvement in project work after key decisions have been taken. These are both legitimate techniques for gathering staff views but they cannot be sold to staff under false pretences.

If your organization does not possess a culture of involvement this does not preclude it from moving in that direction. Allow yourself additional start up time to persuade both staff and management of the reality of the concept. Staff will be cynical and managers will feel threatened as both will feel that they do not have the competencies to work in a participative way. For total staff involvement the following factors must be present:

O   Sharing of all information including what used to be treated as confidential.
O   Shared authority and responsibility.
O   The *how* of change belongs to the workforce while the *what* of change can be strongly influenced from above.
O   Involvement becomes an organizational habit.

The type of organizational team that will live most happily in your organization is explored in detail in Chapter 4.

If you feel that the participative approach will not work in your organization, then do not underestimate the effort and time you need to sell the vision and strategies for change developed by top management. You will still need to involve staff but in more ad hoc ways such as in the detailed implementation of particular aspects of the strategy. Waterman (1982) argues that there are seven interrelated factors that need to be addressed (see Figure 2.2 on page 29). This is often referred to as 'the McKinsey 7s framework'.

Other stakeholders to be considered include customers, shareholders, suppliers and the community. Stakeholders will vary in their ability and desire to influence change depending on the source of their power, which may take a variety of forms:

O   Technical or function skills
O   Legal or policy control
O   Status and/or authority
O   External influence or credibility
O   Control over resources
O   An informal power base

Consumers would see themselves as prime stakeholders where monopoly suppliers provide essential services, such as health, public transport, water, etc. Dynamic organizations would automatically regard customers as stakeholders but customers may not view themselves as such.

You should encourage suppliers to become active stakeholders as they can have a significant impact on design, cost and quality. The same can be said for competitors where alliances could be of mutual benefit. Alliances are explored in greater detail in Chapter 9.

Licence to operate is a concept to be considered with regard to the community as a stakeholder. Polluters of the environment, for example those responsible for the ironization of streams by coal-mines, may lose their 'licence to operate' from the local population if the level of pollution is unacceptable. Where unemployment is not high the levels of acceptability may be raised over time, but when the choice is between pollution and work or no pollution and no work, the local community would support the former. Organizations that are proactive in environmental issues stand to gain a competitive advantage if they introduce improvements before they are compelled to do so by legislation.

To understand the way in which stakeholders may choose to use their influence, carry out a stakeholder analysis of your own organization. The steps to take in stakeholder analysis are as follows:

O   Identify stakeholders – who stands to gain or lose from the changes?
O   Is the impact of change on stakeholders high, medium or low?
O   Who are the main forces for and against change?
O   How much power and influence do they have?
O   Who will actively block or support change?
O   What factors are influencing commitment to change?
O   What can you do to gain support for change and then increase it?
O   What can you do to reduce opposition?

ASSESSING THE FORCES FOR AND AGAINST CHANGE

In order to concentrate effort where it will bring the best return, you need to strengthen the positive factors for change and weaken the negative influences. This approach is called force field analysis and was developed by Kurt Lewin. Clarify the current situation of your own organization and the desired future state that you seek. Then identify the relevant forces within the organization, distinguishing between driving forces that can be seen to facilitate change and restraining forces that might inhibit change. An example of what these forces might include is shown in Figure 2.1. Use Table 2.1 to set out the forces for and against change in your own organization.

Whilst stakeholder and force field analyses are useful tools in planning any organizational change, the action plans developed as a result will work only if managers encourage commitment from the groups and individuals identified. To use this approach follow the steps below:

○   List those individuals/groups who ideally need to support the change.
○   Select from this list those whose support is essential for the change to stand a chance of success.
○   Judge the present level of commitment from each person or group within this critical mass.
○   In each case judge the desired future level of commitment required from them for the proposed change to be successful.

This final step should show who to concentrate on: those people whose commitment needs to increase.

Table 2.2 provides an example of how to plan for stakeholder commitment. The table sets out examples of key stakeholders, their current level of commitment and the extent to which this may need to change. It may be different in your organization. For instance, it may be only possible to increase

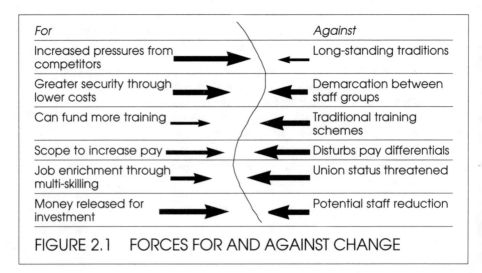

For	Against
Increased pressures from competitors	Long-standing traditions
Greater security through lower costs	Demarcation between staff groups
Can fund more training	Traditional training schemes
Scope to increase pay	Disturbs pay differentials
Job enrichment through multi-skilling	Union status threatened
Money released for investment	Potential staff reduction

FIGURE 2.1   FORCES FOR AND AGAINST CHANGE

TABLE 2.1   FORCES FOR AND AGAINST CHANGE IN YOUR OWN ORGANIZATION

For	Against
1.	
2.	
3.	
4.	

TABLE 2.2   PLANNING STAKEHOLDER COMMITMENT

Key players	Opposition	No commitment	Let it happen	Help it happen	Make it happen
Middle management	x				o
Junior staff		x	o		
Trade unions	x		o		
Shareholders			xo		
Customers		x	o		
Suppliers		x	o		

Key: x – level of commitment at start
o – level of commitment at finish

the commitment of middle managers marginally by 'letting it happen'. If that is the case, you will need to compensate for this by seeking to enlist junior staff to 'help it happen'. Plan the commitment of stakeholders for your own organization by completing Table 2.3.

WHAT NEEDS TO CHANGE

It is often not enough to change only a couple of aspects of an organization. The unchanged features of the organization may hold back the new. McKinsey and

TABLE 2.3   PLANNING THE COMMITMENT OF YOUR
             STAKEHOLDERS

Key players	Opposition	No commitment	Let it happen	Help it happen	Make it happen
Middle management					
Junior staff					
Trade unions					
Shareholders					
Customers					
Suppliers					

Key: x – level of commitment at start
        o – level of commitment at finish

Co. argue that there are seven interrelated factors that need to be addressed (Figure 2.2). Thus an organization wanting to become more customer oriented should be outward looking with a **structure** and **systems** that facilitate a rapid response to their needs. **Staff** should be well motivated with the appropriate **skills** and **values** that stress the importance of customers. All underpinning **strategies** must support and facilitate the change. If one of the main thrusts of the change is a move to teamworking, it would be completely inappropriate to include a large element of individual performance-related pay. The Management **style** is that of facilitator and coach rather than autocrat. These various issues are summarized below.

Strategy

What type of organization do you want yours to be? What are the main steps and milestones along the way to achieving this?

Shared values

Commonly held attitudes that determine behaviour. How do staff feel about working in your organization? Total quality management works through making attention to quality and customer needs values that are shared by all staff.

Style

How do senior managers behave, for instance are they bureaucratic, status conscious or informal?

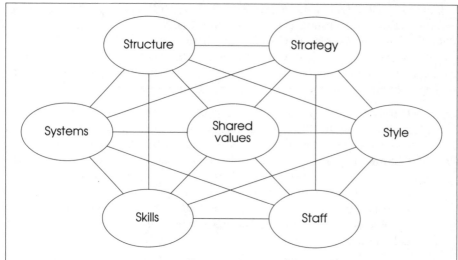

FIGURE 2.2   THE McKINSEY 7s FRAMEWORK
Source: Robert H. Waterman (1982), 'The Seven Elements of
Strategic Fit,' *Journal of Business Strategy*, Vol. 2, No. 3 (Winter),
p. 15.

Structure

How many tiers are there in the organization? Is it based on functional or product management? Are there too many tiers to allow the empowerment of staff to flourish? Is the organization too slow to bring new products to the market because responsibilities are split between different functions?

Systems

These include procedures and routine flows of information, and how information and management technology is used. Monitoring and rewarding staff performance needs to be consistent with other changes.

Skills

Staff competencies. In which areas does the organization excel? What areas need to be strengthened to support the change process and to run the new organization?

Staff

What is the composition of workforce, i.e. professional background; male/female; full-time/part-time; age.

THE CHANGE PROCESS

Many organizations embark on change with near religious zeal and this is often appropriate to harness the energy and enthusiasm to drive the change forward, but acts of blind faith cannot be used in place of more concrete outcome measures if the organization is to test its progress.

One of the problems of introducing change is that it may have only a temporary effect. People may want to retreat to their comfort zone and revert to their old behaviour. Kurt Lewin (1947, 1951) proposed three steps necessary to achieve permanent change: unfreezing; changing; refreezing.

O   **Unfreezing** takes place when people feel their behaviour has become unrewarding and they are willing to learn new approaches, e.g. when employees see their job security threatened by a competitor.

O   **Change** happens when people try out new behaviours. They may require a great deal of support to reduce their feelings of discomfort; the use of 'safe' training environments can help.

O   **Refreezing** occurs when staff internalize new behaviours that then become second nature. Rewarding people with praise and money will help sustain the changes.

In today's environment behaviours will not be refrozen for long as there is a need for continuous change. Whilst staff are expected to internalize new behaviours these should be assessed and reassessed to test whether they are still appropriate. Successful organizations are like chameleons – they quickly adapt themselves and their staff to their ever-changing environment.

Project management is needed throughout the change management process to link and synchronize the many aspects of the evolving strategy, such as research and development, production, staff involvement and job design. The implication should not be that you should form an elite group to design your change strategy behind closed doors, rather that competencies such as planning, scheduling and resource allocation should be available at all levels.

Appropriate timing involves finding the right balance between the quick fix solution and the process being so protracted that enthusiasm is lost. Free up staff time so that staff can give change the priority it deserves.

UNPRODUCTIVE GENUINE CHANGE

Some organizations seek to avoid the pain of change by doing only the minimum to accommodate new pressures. This superficial reaction is called first order change. It is what the French mean by 'plus ça change, plus c'est la même chose', or 'the more it changes the more it remains the same'. This is change within a given system. What you need to achieve is *second order* change. It is a more fundamental change resulting in a new system being adopted. It is a discontinuous break with the past (Watzlawick *et al.*, 1974, p. 10).

The difference between the two can be illustrated by the way computers have been used. For a long time they were an example of first order change. Organizations used them as 'super clerks' to work faster than their human counterparts, but they made little impact on the wider organization, costs or customer benefits. An example of second order change is when computerized tills were introduced into supermarkets. When an item is scanned at the checkout

TABLE 2.4   SUCCESS AND FAILURE FACTORS FOR CHANGE

Factors	Success	Failure
Responsibility	Commitment from the top	Devolved too far down the organization
Direction	Clear vision reinforced by actions of top management	Don't do as I do, do as I say!
Consistent strategies	New and existing strategies support each other	New and existing strategies in conflict with each other
Project management	Competencies available at all levels	Inadequate provision
Timescale	Long-term commitment	Quick fix
Resources	Staff time freed up for change activities	Another objective added to a long list
Communication	Free flow in all directions	Information is power
Training and development	Training for all on a regular basis	Training for top people when they want it
Staff participation	We solve problems together	We tell you the solutions, you carry them out
Attitude to change	Change is an opportunity, let's have more of it	Phew, I've survived that change, now I can get back to normal
Evaluation	Before and after evaluation of all key factors including customers	Act of faith – no monitoring

the till not only rings up the bill, but also initiates a replacement order. Thus a completely new way of working has been introduced, which eliminates manual stock checking, a slower and less accurate process that resulted in the occasional empty shelf.

SUCCESS AND FAILURE FACTORS FOR CHANGE

Table 2.4 sets out factors commonly associated with success and failure. Use it as a guide rather than a gospel. Thinking about when change was last introduced

TABLE 2.5   SUCCESS AND FAILURE FACTORS FOR CHANGE IN YOUR ORGANIZATION

Factors	Success	Failure
Responsibility		
Direction		
Consistent strategies		
Project management		
Timescale		
Resources		
Communication		
Training and development		
Staff participation		
Attitude to change		
Evaluation		

in your organization, how many of the success factors were present? What about the failure factors? What do you need to do differently this time around? Complete Table 2.5 for your own organization.

CHECKLIST FOR MANAGEMENT ACTION

1.   What are the chief risks associated with change for your organization? List them below:

2.   What will be the role of top management for change? Write a brief for them.
3.   How will you involve staff? Describe at least three methods that would work in your organization.
4.   How supportive are the seven interrelated factors that comprise your organizational culture? Make sure that you have completed the McKinsey 7s table on page 29. Any conflicts identified must be pursued, as all underpinning strategies must support and facilitate change.
5.   Identify your principal stakeholders and their likely commitment to change. Use Tables 2.1 and 2.3 to do this.
6.   Using the force field analysis of your own organization made in Table 2.2, and the information from Table 2.3, decide how you are going to overcome the forces against change and strengthen the forces for change to gain commitment from your key stakeholders.
7.   Determine the success and failure factors for change that are currently present in your organization, using the table on page 26 to help you. What are you going to do to lessen the failure factors and build on the success factors? You will have already detailed some solutions in your answer to question 4.

PART II

THE FUTURE

If a man will begin with certainties, he shall end in
doubts, but if he will be content to begin with doubts,
he shall end in certainties.

Francis Bacon, 1605

3

VISION AND BEYOND

The best way to predict the future is to invent it.

Alan Kay, Atari

SCANNING YOUR HORIZONS

Where do you start? It is tempting to rush in to making changes to your products and services, which you know so well. But it is not wise to embark on the journey of change without a clear idea of where you are heading. Otherwise there is a real danger that you will bring about first order change rather than the more effective and fundamental second order change. The history of change management is littered with examples of those who increased their efficiency in producing goods and services that were no longer required. We are sure you do not want to be remembered in this way. So instead, pause, and jump into your helicopter to see the big picture, for 'If a man does not know to which port he is sailing, no wind is favourable'. Seneca. This is where political, economic, social and technical (PEST) analysis comes in.

Political changes such as privatization have created opportunities for the private sector to diversify, for example Group 4 moved into prisoner escort duties. The road building programme of the Conservative government has boosted that industry. The proposal to privatize the railways led to a massive drop in the sales of rolling stock as British Rail sought to improve its immediate cash position to enhance its attractiveness to potential purchasers.

Economic changes such as increased wealth have led to the rapid growth of huge, out of town shopping complexes made possible by increased car ownership. A corresponding decline has occurred in some of the traditional, city shopping areas. Increased affluence combined with lower production costs has led to many 'disposable' goods, which are cheaper to replace than repair.

Social change is exemplified by the impact of the post-war population bulge. It provided the critical mass of the youth market for the pop music industry in the 1960s, the flat market in the 1970s and the house market in the 1980s. Social factors are most powerful when they interact with other factors. Thus the youth market was also supported by economic prosperity. The housing market of the 1980s was also fuelled by mortgage relief subsidies, a political policy to expand

37

home ownership substantially. An ageing population drawing good occupational pensions for the former high earners has led to a new affluent, leisured group. The travel company Saga is geared exclusively to the needs of this market. The high participation in the workforce of women with family commitments led to a massive growth of labour saving goods in the home, later to be followed by a growth in production of convenience foods. The green movement was instrumental in ending the use of environmentally harmful CFC gases in aerosols.

Technical changes such as cheaper and more powerful computers have supported the rise of telephone banking and insurance. The speed of applying knowledge is ever more critical as it becomes rapidly obsolete, one of the factors influencing some organizations to invest more in the skills of their workforces. It also increases the importance of research and development.

In Figure 3.1 we demonstrate the range of a PEST analysis which we have completed for a pharmaceutical company. Now carry out this exercise for your own organization. In each box, list those factors either positive or negative that you feel will impact on your organization in the next five years.

This PEST analysis will begin to give you a bird's-eye view of the landscape in which your organization is operating. Particularly be aware of the negative factors that protrude like rocky crags and could hole your organization irreparably. Your ability to navigate around the landscape will depend on the strengths and weaknesses within your organization and on what other threats and opportunities it has to steer a course around. It is important, therefore, that in tandem with the PEST analysis you also carry out a SWOT analysis. This is an analysis of the organization's strengths, weaknesses, opportunities and threats. (This is explored in more detail on page 44.)

Political	Economic
− increased regulation − capping of drug expenditure − increased testing requirements prior to licensing − limiting the scope of patents + possible change of government	− key revenue earning drugs no longer protected by patents
+ increase in elderly population + higher expectations of healthcare + patients' charter of rights − move to homeopathic remedies	+ increased use of robotics and automation + substitution of synthetic raw materials
Social	Technical

FIGURE 3.1   PEST ANALYSIS OF A PHARMACEUTICAL COMPANY

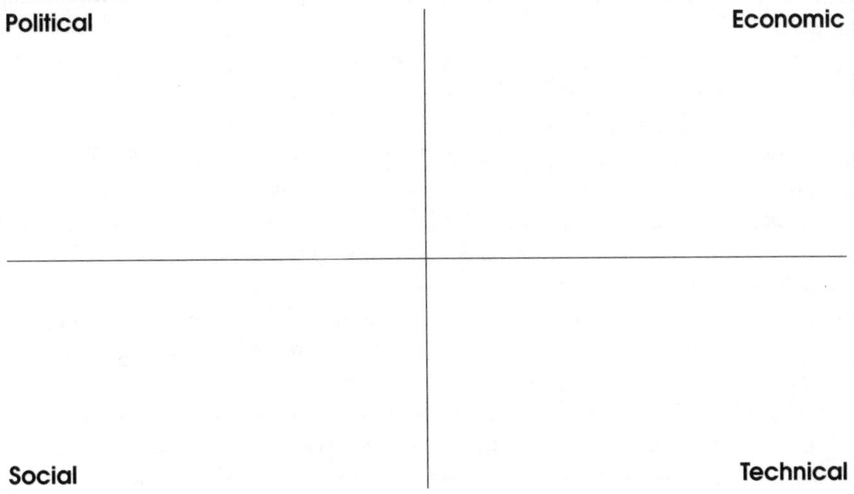

Political		Economic
Social		Technical

FIGURE 3.2   PEST ANALYSIS OF YOUR OWN
                          ORGANIZATION

IDENTIFYING AND ANALYSING YOUR CORE COMPETENCIES

You now know that no organization is safe or immune from threats to its survival, so what do you do about it? First, find out what you are really good at and why. Define your core competencies, a much harder task than it may at first seem. For instance, would you define Marks and Spencer as a good retailer and then stop there. The reality is that it has excellent financial systems to establish the return on each square metre of retail space. It can then quickly give more space to fast-moving lines at the expense of less popular items. It is also an expert in managing suppliers through building close relationships. These relationships are based on the joint development of products and processes that must conform to clearly defined quality standards, which may explain Marks and Spencer's success in expanding into the new area of food and wine. Marks and Spencer's core competencies can therefore be defined as financial control systems, supplier development and management, one reason, perhaps, why it used to steer clear of the high fashion market, which places a much greater premium on style.

To get a good understanding of your strengths and weaknesses you need to compare yourself with your competition along a whole range of dimensions. A useful approach is to define your customers and competitors and search out your core competencies in relationship to them.

Define your customers. Are their needs very different? Find out from the customers themselves if there is scope to tailor specific products to each submarket? Even Levi Strauss, the jeans manufacturer, suffered some unwelcome shocks when it asked the following questions of its customers, i.e. the retailers who sold its products:

O   What did they the retailers need to be successful?
O   Who were their best suppliers?
O   How did Levi Strauss compare?

Levi Strauss was praised for its excellent design and successful marketing, its core competencies, but its customers had to remind it that they could not make a living from selling empty space on shelves. Levi Strauss' supply capability left much to be desired. This example shows how an internal process can let an organization down.

You can search out your core competencies by working through the framework illustrated in Table 3.1. We have completed this exercise for a successful fast-moving consumer goods company.

Your can use Table 3.2 to complete the exercise for your own organization. How safe is your organization? How many of your competencies are unique? How many are invested in the hands and minds of a few key individuals? What are you doing to ensure that these competencies are maintained and developed over time? What do you do to determine the competencies of your main competitors to see what you can learn from them. The market-place has a number of organizational wrecks of those who lost or failed to maintain their core competencies. Do this analysis to ensure that you are not one of them.

We now need to look at opportunities and threats. The opportunity in our Marks and Spencer example was the potential for growth in the convenience food market. Threats could come from a new entrant to your market who successfully rewrites the rules on how business is done. It could be that your market is about to be attacked by a lower cost producer from the Pacific Rim. Another type of threat is replacement, for example the electric office typewriter was undermined by the dedicated wordprocessor, which in turn has been replaced by the microcomputer running a wordprocessing package. What are you not good at? Can you stop doing it or would it better to get someone else to supply it for you? In this way you can reduce some of the potential threats.

Another way of discovering your opportunities and threats is by analysing your products and services to determine which are the stars, cash cows, problem children and dogs (Figure 3.3). The **stars** enjoy the best of all worlds being the products or businesses with increasing market share in a growing market. The **problem children** are in the right market, a growing one, but are not doing too well there. This situation is worth trying to turn around once you know where it is being held back, be it in quality, price or both. This sort of **dog** has had its day and sadly it ought to be put down. **Cash cows** provide steady income, which is fine providing they are not nurtured at the expense of future stars. Money now rather than money in the future can be very seductive to risk-averse organizations.

Your next step is to examine cost and quality in greater detail, reviewing each individual component of a product to clarify what you should keep in-house and what you should out source (Figure 3.4). The really nimble organizations are those that are not weighed down by activities in which they do not excel.

TABLE 3.1   IDENTIFYING AND ANALYSING CORE COMPETENCIES

Factor	Design	Marketing	Logistics	Cost control	Flexible production processes	Skilled workforce
Essential to corporate survival in the short and long term	Yes	Yes	Yes	Yes	Yes	Yes
Invisible to competitors	No	No	Yes	Yes	Yes	Yes
Difficult to imitate	No	No	Yes	No	No	No
Unique to the corporation	No	No	No	No	No	No
A mix of skill, resources and processes	No	Yes	Yes	Yes	Yes	Yes
A capability which the organization can sustain over time	Yes	Yes	Yes	Yes	Yes	Yes
Greater than the competence of an individual	Yes	Yes	Yes	Yes	Yes	Yes
Essential to the development of core products and eventually to end products	Yes	Yes	No	Yes	Yes	Yes
Essential to the implementation of the strategic vision of the corporation	Yes	Yes	Yes?	No	Yes	Yes
Essential to the strategic decisions of the corporation	No	Yes	No	No	Yes?	Yes

Source: Mahen Tampoe, 'Exploiting the Core Competencies of Your Organisation', *Long Range Planning*, Vol. 27, August 1994, pp. 68 and 69.

TABLE 3.2   IDENTIFYING AND ANALYSING YOUR CORE COMPETENCIES

Factor	Design	Marketing	Logistics	Cost control	Flexible production processes	Skilled workforce
Essential to corporate survival in the short and long term						
Invisible to competitors						
Difficult to imitate						
Unique to the corporation						
A mix of skill, resources and processes						
A capability which the organization can sustain over time						
Greater than the competence of an individual						
Essential to the development of core products and eventually to end products						
Essential to the implementation of the strategic vision of the corporation						
Essential to the strategic decisions of the corporation						

Market share

		High	Low
Market growth rate	**High**	Star	Question mark (or problem child)
	Low	Cash Cow	Dog

FIGURE 3.3   IDENTIFYING YOUR WINNING AND LOSING
PRODUCTS

Source: Gerry Johnson and Kevan Scholes (1988) *Exploring Corporate Strategy*, 2nd edition, London: Prentice-Hall. (Original source: C. Hofer and D. Schedel (1978), the Boston Consulting Group Matrix, *Strategic Formulation: Analytical Concepts*, West Publishing Co.

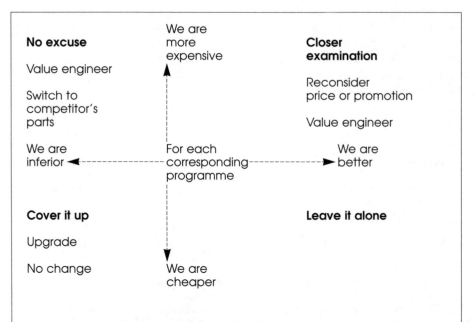

FIGURE 3.4   REVIEWING STRATEGY FOR EACH
COMPONENT OR PRODUCT

Source: Kenichi Ohmae (1986), *The Mind of the Strategist*, Harmondsworth: Penguin, p. 26 (copyright McGraw-Hill Inc. 1982)

Paradise, but only for the time being, is where a component you produce is both better and cheaper than the competition. At the other extreme, if your component is poor in quality and more expensive, drastic action is required. You could out source it from a competitor or try to reduce the cost through value engineering. Quality will need to be improved as well once its cause is discovered. Where you are better in quality but higher cost, one option would be to convince your customers to pay for a premium quality. Car manufacturers can do this where their cars have high resale values in the second-hand market. An advertising campaign for a beer, Stella Artois, emphasized its high price and questioned provocatively whether the consumers were in its class. If you cannot convince customers to pay a premium price, then you need to go down the cost reduction path. Where you are inferior and cheaper you ought to upgrade your product although, if you have many other pressing priorities, it could remain unchanged for a while.

From these analyses you should be able to draw a SWOT chart for your organization. To help you do this, we have completed one for the same pharmaceutical company that we used in the PEST analysis (Figure 3.1). Use Figure 3.6 to produce a SWOT chart for your own organization.

As with force field analysis you want to build on the pluses and see how you can overcome the minuses. The information from this analysis will be fundamental to forming your vision of the future. Now you have been on your helicopter ride, you should have a pretty good idea of the terrain below and should be able to develop a perspective of where you would ideally like your organization to be situated. This view becomes your vision, so that you can move your organization forward to this new place. You need to be able to describe what it looks like, what it feels like and what it will be like when your organization gets there.

Strengths	Weaknesses
+ research and development	– high research and development costs
+ highly skilled workforce	– core competencies in research in heads of a few key staff
+ strong global operation	– too many cash cows due for slaughter
+ take-over potential within own country	– possible take-over by larger foreign companies
+ R&D on the way to finding a cancer cure	– a leading competitor will market its cancer products first
Opportunities	Threats

FIGURE 3.5   SWOT ANALYSIS

Strengths	Weaknesses
+	−
+	−
+	−
+	−
+	−
+	−
+	−
+	−
+	−
+	−
Opportunities	Threats

FIGURE 3.6   SWOT ANALYSIS OF YOUR ORGANIZATION

WHY HAVE A VISION?

A 'vision is the difference between short-term moves to improve the bottom line [like assets, sales or cuts in the r & d budget] and long term change. Vision translates strategies you might have on paper into a way of life' (Belasco, 1990).

Stephen Connock (1991, p. 2) lists the following main features of vision:

O   It will be cohesive, providing a common thread through business mission and subsequent strategies.
O   It will be specific enough to provide direction yet general enough to remain relevant despite fluctuations in conditions in the short term.
O   It will be inspiring, aiming at 'excellence' as defined by the organization.
O   It will describe the core values strongly held by the organization.
O   It will provide a yardstick by which to judge the future performance of the organization.

Do you recognize the following?

O   Inconsistent objectives throughout the organization.
O   Staff pulling in different directions.
O   A contradiction between short-term and long-term objectives.
O   An obsession with the here and now.

O   An organization drifting from crisis to crisis.

What is needed is a vision to cement the organization together, to give the organization forward direction and to measure its progress along that path. How will you get there if you don't know where you are going? A vision allows an organization to go beyond modest targets to take on big challenges which need significant amounts of planning and preparation. A vision acts as a lynch pin for organizational objectives. People will be committed to pull together if they share a vision of the future.

❖   **Health warning**

No vision no future.

CREATING A VISION

The creation of a vision has been described as a 'mental journey from the known to the unknown, creating the future from a montage of current facts, hopes, dreams, dangers and opportunities'. Creating a vision will always start at the top, although they may be legitimized by involving staff and other stakeholders in their formulation. Visions which are created further down the organization will be realized if they are sponsored from the top or if they involve only marginal, localized change. Drawing on your analysis of the environment, your customers, your competitors and the capability within your organization, your strategic vision must take into account the synergy between these factors.

Review your PEST and SWOT analyses. You need to ask yourself the following types of questions:

O   Where does your organization add maximum value?
O   What are its strategic advantages?
O   What are the opportunities for your organization?
O   What could you do for your customers that would put you way ahead of the opposition?
O   How can you get the staff to sign up?
O   Do you involve the staff in creating the vision, and how?

Visions that are shaped using the past and the present lend themselves to the active participation of the whole organization. An example of this is the incremental change made over the last twenty-five years by Sainsbury's, whereby it has moved from small grocery shops to large, out-of-town supermarkets. To avoid resistance it is vital to use the expertise and values within the organization to form the foundation on which to construct the new vision.

Some visions imply such radical change that there is no basis within the organization from which to construct the new. Some employers have not involved staff where technologies, competencies and ways of working may be obsolete. A good example of this is the demise of the printing industry in Fleet

Street when the introduction of new technology and methods of working was achieved by opening up greenfield sites. This approach is clearly expensive as it involves some double running costs and major disruption of employee relations. Confrontation is not the only route as we showed in the Thorn EMI case study in Chapter 2.

At the other end of the spectrum are search conferences. This method involves as many people as possible, drawn ideally from all the stakeholders, in the design of a shared vision. Marvin Weisbord in his book *Discovering Common Ground* (1992) describes it as 'a creative interplay between two key strategic decisions: who gets to be there and what they actually do'. In these meetings 'who' is everybody with a stake in the meeting's outcome, which usually involves a cross-section of the whole system under discussion and may include employees from all levels as well as customers, clients and suppliers. Instead of solving problems piecemeal, they scan whole systems together. Everyone gets the view from the top. The checklist at the end of this chapter, describes how to organize a search conference.

Most visions will incorporate changes which lie between these two extremes. Generally such radical change is needed because the organization has failed to make incremental change in the past.

Many organizations have created the vision using the input of senior managers only. Its impact on the organization is lost as staff fail to sign up to the vision. It is more successful in the long term to involve staff in the creation of the vision in spite of the considerable investment in the short term.

MISSION STATEMENTS

A mission statement embodies in written form the ethos of the vision. It should be supported by a statement of value to which the organization aspires. Unfortunately, mission statements often degenerate into a set of platitudes that are so all-encompassing as to be almost meaningless. Is yours unique? Too many are interchangeable. Many organizations could swop mission statements and no one would recognize the difference. A whole industry has grown up on developing such statements. Rather than sounding slick and memorable, the mission statement should be built on the primary purpose of the organization and represent something that all stakeholders can recognize and subscribe to.

Your vision must be grounded in the reality of the assessments that you have made about your organization and the environment within which it operates. You must make sure that the gap is not too large between where you are now and where your vision places your organization in the future. Do you have the capability in your organization to achieve the vision or should you buy it in or form an alliance to strengthen your organization? You also need to check your vision, particularly if it has been formed in a less participative way, with all your major stakeholders to ensure that it aligns with their perceptions. Ambitious visions are fine, unachievable ones will serve no purpose as a guiding light.

Once you have produced your vision, it must not be written on tablets of stone or else it could become the organization's tombstone. Visions must be kept alive by constant updating. Staff at all levels, not just the strategic level, should be scanning the environment to pick up hints and titbits of information that may impact in any way. The organization must become more extrovert and less centralized so that its vision can evolve and adapt to lead its way through the changes that will become a way of life.

At this point in the book you know from the analyses that you completed in Chapters 1 and 2 the current position of your organization. Chapter 3 has assisted you in developing a vision of where you want your organization to be in the future. The task facing you now is how to get from where you are to where you want to be. In Chapters 4, 5 and 6 we lead you through the maze of ideas surrounding empowerment, TQM and business process re-engineering. Chapter 7 looks at a pick and mix option which incorporates aspects of all three approaches. Armed with this knowledge you will be able to select the best route for your organizational journey.

CHECKLIST FOR MANAGEMENT ACTION

1.   Environmental scanning
     Using the PEST analysis you will have assessed what changes in your wider environment will be to your advantage. Now you need to consider how to maximize them, by harnessing and developing the organization's capabilities. You will need to bear in mind other wider changes that may be to your disadvantage. It may be wise to withdraw from those activities which will be made vulnerable by these external changes before they become unrewarding. You should redirect their resources to where they will bring a better return.

2.   Customer audit
     O   What do your customers think of you?

3.   Competitive analysis
     O   What do your competitors do to attract customers that you do not?
     O   In which critical processes are your competitors better and why?

4.   Capability analysis
     O   What are your core competencies?

5.   Identify your winning and losing products, i.e. stars, cash cows, problem children and dogs.

6.   Carry out a SWOT analysis to discover the organization's internal landscape.

7.   On the strength of all the above information, develop your vision. Search conferences are one method of developing a vision in a highly participative way. They are based on the following principles:

     a)   They must involve the largest possible number of people with a stake in the organization's future – staff, customers, suppliers, managers, union leaders, etc.
     b)   The work of the conference must be self-managed by the participants.
     c)   Participants complete five tasks:
          O   examining the past (strengths and weaknesses);
          O   looking at the present in terms of global trends;
          O   looking at what the company is proud of and what it is sorry about in its present state;
          O   creating ideal future scenarios for 5–25 years hence;
          O   making action plans for the short and long term.
     d)   Participants then examine the present from two perspectives:
          O   the external events and trends shaping the future right now;
          O   the internal strengths, needs and hopes of the organization.
     e)   Finally, people make three lists suggesting actions for themselves, for their functions and for the whole organization.
     f)   The lists are reviewed, drawn into a cohesive vision and an action plan agreed for the achievement of the vision over the appropriate timescale, i.e. with some short- and long-term goals.

g) The ground rules for the whole process are:
- O all ideas are valid;
- O every task must produce output;
- O all data must be put on flip charts;
- O no problem solving is allowed;
- O groups are responsible for finishing on time.

PART III

OPTIONS FOR CHANGE

Those who are going to be in business tomorrow are
those who understand that the future, as always,
belongs to the brave.
William Bernbach, Doyle Dane Bernbach credo

4

STAFF EMPOWERMENT

Power corrupts, but lack of power corrupts absolutely.
Adlai Stevenson

Never tell people how to do things. Tell them what to
do and they will surprise you with their ingenuity.
General George S. Patton

By now you should not only be committed to change but also have a clear vision of what your future might be. This vision will have been either drawn up by the top team and extensively marketed to the rest of the stakeholders or developed from basic principles using the wealth of ideas and experience of all your principal stakeholders. You must check the organizational reality of the commitment to the vision. It is easy at this stage to be seduced by the determination to reach the next milestone on the plan instead of ensuring that you are taking the rest of the organization with you.

Now that you have confirmed that you have commitment, which strategy will you use to deliver the vision? There are at least three main routes: empowerment, total quality management and re-engineering. In addition, there are routes which consist of elements of all three of these. We will help you decide which approach suits your organization by examining empowerment in this chapter and looking in depth at TQM in Chapter 5 and re-engineering in Chapter 6.

Empowerment is a central route in that it can be used as a main pathway in itself or to support other approaches. No change can be successfully implemented without some degree of staff involvement, whether this be throughout the whole process or agreeing new working practices at the end of the change cycle. The underlying premise behind empowerment is that promoting employee involvement enables workers to perform as whole, thinking human beings. Through empowerment the strength of the whole workforce is harnessed and used most effectively to meet customer requirements with improved quality products and services.

The Japanese philosophy that has been so successful, is also extremely straightforward and all the more powerful for it – get the design of the products right, empower the employees to run and continuously improve these processes, and quality and profits will follow naturally. This philosophy, however, demonstrates the difference in thinking between Western and Japanese managers, i.e. Western managers believe that bosses do the thinking and workers carry out the tasks. The Japanese believe that only by drawing upon the combined brain power of all its employees can a firm face up to the changes required in the future. The Japanese also spend much more time on the initial phase of a project. They make up time during the implementation phase as the consensus they have built allows them to complete the process without major resistance.

WHAT WILL EMPOWERMENT DO?

Empowerment can increase and at worst maintain your competitiveness. Robert and Marie Ripley (1992) list the following effects of empowerment:

1.   It reduces mistakes by increasing the motivation of employees to take more responsibility for their own actions. Under TQM the responsibility for quality is passed to the front-line worker and the traditional role of supervisor is changed to a facilitator.
2.   It increases the opportunity for creativity and innovation. Internally, the worker is encouraged to find new ways of working that can reduce costs through greater efficiency or increase sales by improving the product.
3.   It promotes continuous assessment and therefore improvement of process, product and service.
4.   It improves customer satisfaction by having the employee closest to the customer make rapid, relevant decisions. Staff are empowered to deal with customer problems as they arise without reference to higher authority.
5.   It increases employee loyalty, while at the same time, through peer pressure, reducing turnover, absenteeism and illness.
6.   It increases productivity because employees spend less time waiting for others to make decisions. This is an important aspect of re-engineering (see Chapter 6).
7.   Self-management of work procedures and resources such as rostering gives employees more involvement and control.
8.   Fewer management layers are required as empowerment relieves upper and middle management of purely 'control' tasks.

The true value of empowerment is revealed in a number of working examples. Perhaps one of the most significant is that of Bayamon, part of General Electric. As related by Thomas A. Stewart in *Fortune* magazine (1993), the company increased the productivity of its workforce by 20 per cent in one year by empowering that workforce. It delayered its organization into only three layers. All the workers were organized into teams that owned part of the work. These were facilitated by an adviser. Team members were drawn from all parts of the plant. Bayamon became a perpetual learning machine with hourly paid workers changing jobs every six months. All workers were rewarded on the basis of skill, knowledge and business performance. Another well-known example is that of

Case study: Empowerment – Semco, Sao Paulo, Brazil

Semco moved from a traditional, hierarchical organization 12 years ago to one of participative management. It became number one or two in each of its markets. Productivity increased nearly sevenfold between 1980 and 1993. $2.2 million profit was earned in the 18 months following the introduction of participation. Semco won a national award for labour relations in 1989. No one left the company in a period of 14 months and it had a backlog of 2000 job applications. Its factories increased in number from one to six and its employees increased from 100 to 830.

To achieve these staggering results, Semco took the following actions:

○   It sacked the old management who were against diversification.
○   It dispensed with secretaries, everyone does their own photo-copying and types letters.
○   It ended the dress code.
○   It allowed meeting rooms to be used by staff for social functions.
○   It threw out rules and procedures.
○   It delayered; fewer managers are needed as staff make their own decisions.
○   Financial information is openly discussed, with all books open.
○   It reduced head office staff by 75 per cent.

Staff were empowered to perform the following roles:

○   Set their own production quotas.
○   Help design new products.
○   Contribute to the marketing plan.
○   Recruit and promote all staff in the work area.
○   Assess managers every six months with the results put on display.
○   Decide on factory relocation (the factory was closed for the day to visit sites).

The ethos of the new organization is reflected in the following:

Three stone cutters were asked about their jobs. The first said he was paid to cut stones. The second replied that he used special techniques to shape stones in an exceptional way. The third stone cutter smiled and said: I build cathedrals (p. 42).

Source: Ricardo Semler (1993), *MAVERICK!* London: Century

Semco, which is described above. Both of these cases illustrate the need for staff involvement, management support, staff information, appropriate training and compatible organizational systems. These essential ingredients are discussed in more detail later in this chapter.

THE REALITY OF EMPOWERMENT

The degree of 'empowerment' observable in organizations can be very varied. Sometimes the word is used merely in place of consultation – David Bowen and Edward Lawler (1992) term this *'suggestion involvement'*. The fast food chain McDonald's uses this form of very limited 'empowerment'. A second type of empowerment is called *job involvement* by Bowen and Lawler. This form entails extensive job design, so that employees use a variety of skills and often work in teams. They have a considerable degree of freedom in deciding how to carry out their work. However, higher level strategic decisions about organizational structure, power and the reward strategy remain the responsibility of senior management.

The third type of empowerment is *high involvement*, often found in the horizontal style organization as described by Rosabeth Moss Kanter in her speech to the 1992 conference of the Institute of Personnel Development (Golzen, 1992). Here all information on business performance is shared horizontally across the organization, as well as up and down the delayered structure. Employees develop extensive skills in team work, problem solving and business operations.

Edward Lawler III, Director of the Center for Effective Organizations at the University of Southern California, assesses in his latest book *Employee Involvement and Total Quality Management* (1992) the level of activity with regard to empowerment in the Fortune 1000 top American companies:

> In a nutshell, it says that a lot of people are doing a little bit. Just about every company has something it calls employee involvement or total quality management. But in almost all cases, it's a small part of the workforce that's involved.

The reality is that there is no single approach that is ideal in every industry, company, function or situation. Like so many other management ideas, the ideal degree and form of empowerment depends on circumstances. For example, high involvement empowerment is essential for TQM, but job involvement and suggestion involvement can be used for business process re-engineering and pick and mix. Table 4.1 considers the most suitable type of empowerment in relation to different types of organization.

TABLE 4.1   WHAT TYPE OF EMPOWERMENT IS MOST SUITED TO YOUR ORGANIZATION?

Type of organization	Type of involvement
Traditional, vertical hierarchical: highly proscribed working practices and procedures	Suggestion involvement – consultation
Delayering organization: strategic decision making still with managers	Job involvement
Horizontal organization: information share up, down and across	High involvement

TABLE 4.2   THE CHANGES NEEDED FOR EMPOWERMENT

From low empowerment	1	2	3	4	5	To high empowerment
Technology first						People first
People as spare parts						People as valuable resources
Control						Commitment
Procedures book						Self control
Many levels						Flat organization
Autocratic style						Participative style
Directive decision making (one person decides)						Consensus decision making (group decides)
Competitive						Cooperative
'Tell me what to do'						'How can we work better'
'It's only a job'						'It's my job'
Skilled in one job						Constantly learning
Low risk taking						Innovation
Reacting to change (reactive)						Seizing opportunities (proactive)
Stability and predictability						Constant change
'We'll think about it and set up a committee to study it'						Do it faster than the competition
Internal organization driven						Customer driven
Rule bound and slow						Flexible and fast
Doing things right						Doing the right things
'I only work here'						'I am the company'
Power over workers (told what to do)						Empowered workforce (able to do what is right)
If it's not broken don't fix it						Constant improvement
Acceptable quality and service (good enough)						World-class quality (The best)

Source: Adapted from Bob Harper and Ann Harper (1989), *Succeeding as a Self-Directed Work Team*, New York: MW Corporation

Before introducing the concept of empowerment, you need to check how motivated and involved your staff currently are. Table 4.2 (see page 57) shows the cultural extremes between unempowered and empowered organizations. Use it as an audit tool within your own organization before and after you complete your empowerment programme. Fill it in by putting an 'n' for where you are now in the appropriate column and an 'f' for where you want to be in the future. You will then be able to see the amount by which you want to change.

THE VITAL INGREDIENTS OF EMPOWERMENT

❖   **Health warning +**

The vital ingredients that follow must be selected according to the type of empowerment that will work readily in your organization without substantial structural changes.

1. EMPLOYEE INVOLVEMENT

To improve quality and productivity, and to make themselves more competitive, some organizations have established self-directed teams. Such teams are generally considered too counter-cultural and receive too much management opposition to prove successful in the traditional, hierarchical organization. It must be remembered that it is staff involvement that is the important principle and this can be achieved to a lesser extent through quality circles and project teams. A comparison of these approaches is outlined in Table 4.3.

If we relate this comparison back to the degree of involvement in your own organization, you will see that self-managing teams will work only where there is high involvement, project teams require job involvement and quality circles need only suggestion involvement. Make sure that you have audited the level of involvement in your own organization so that you can decide whether empowerment is the way forward to change for you.

2. MANAGEMENT SUPPORT

Not keeping your management and organizational style up to date can result in traumatic, chaotic changes rather than the smoother incremental changes made by more progressive organizations. Constructive change, which is needed to remain 'state of the art' in management, can be brought about only if management truly wants it, is willing to change its own style and organization and works on the basics.

In his book *Rebirth of the Corporation* D. Quinn Mills (1992) reports that he sees three management styles in use today, and that they are competing with one another. The first is the traditional style where managers:

a)   Organize, i.e. decide what's to be done, split it into tasks, and decide who's to do the tasks.

TABLE 4.3   TYPES OF ORGANIZATIONAL TEAM

Dimensions	Self-managing team	Quality circle	Project team
Status	The way the business is managed	Mostly in mature companies	Put together temporarily on a one-time basis
Life expectancy	Permanent structure	Permanent or temporary	Disbanded once project over
Ease of start up	Start up more difficult and lengthy	Moderate in ease and speed of start up	Easier start up
Participation	Not voluntary but individual participation levels vary	Usually voluntary	Usually assigned or sometimes voluntary
Membership	Entire work group	A sub-set of the work group	Drawn from several work groups
Leadership	May be elected or appointed by management	Internal leader elected or external leader appointed by management	Appointed by management
Type of problem solving	Today's issues selected from a wide range	Problems tackled one at a time, usually a larger issue for a long period selected from a wide range	One task or project within a timeframe
Degree of delegation	Shared authority and responsibility to fulfil mission and make recommendations	Usually give recommendations, sometimes implement	Project leader has authority for reporting and recommendations
Motivational impact	Strong	Moderate to strong	Moderate, dependent on time, visibility and competitive incentive
Position	Largely replaces existing organization	An overlay on the existing organization	An overlay on the existing organization
Training required	Multi-activity and cross-functionally trained team members	Not necessarily related to current job skill	Group specialists banded together on temporary basis
Authority levels	Executives retain authority over the what (strategies). Team assumes authority on the how (tactics)	No change	No change
Skills required	Team skills, self-management, interpersonal skills, problem solving, maintenance skills, project management	Team skills, creativity, problem solving, maintenance skills	Team skills, project management, team processes, maintenance skills

Source: Robert E. Ripley and Marie J. Ripley (1992), 'Empowerment, the Cornerstone of Quality: Empowering Management in Innovative Organisations in the 1990s', *Management Decision*, Vol. 30, No. 4, pp. 20–43

b)   Deputize, i.e. assign responsibility for the tasks to an individual, a department, a division and a subsidiary.

c)   Supervise, i.e. see that the tasks are carried out on schedule in an appropriate way.

The second style is really the traditional one again, but carried out participatively rather than autocratically, i.e. participation mechanisms such as quality circles are used.

The third style that is evolving is empowerment. In place of organizing the work the manager articulates a mission, i.e. a specific objective at the work unit level, to be accomplished within a certain time. Instead of deputizing the manager empowers individuals or a team to accomplish the mission in the way they think is best, with the resources that are available. In place of supervision, the manager measures results against the mission.

Many organizations are currently confusing this kind of management with directive, participative management, where the culture of command and control remains firmly in place but people are ordered to participate in limited decision making. They are told they are being empowered when, in fact, they are not. Empowerment is not real unless people understand the mission and have some means of measuring their performance against it. These two managerial responsibilities are hard to carry out. Managers have difficulty in expressing a mission in language that helps people to understand and make it effective. Managers must not fall back on the old supervisory measure of success meaning that orders were carried out. When people do not feel responsible for results, they also don't feel responsible for the effort and performance of the task.

The three main areas in which managers must act if they are to move the organization from a traditional, mechanical one to a more horizontally oriented organization with self-managed work groups have been identified by Sigvard Rubenowitz (1992):

O   They must pay attention simultaneously to the three strategic aspects: the steering system of the technological and administrative frameworks; the organizational structure; and interpersonal relationships.

O   They must be aware of the need for training of their subordinates at the transition.

O   They must realize the radical change in the role of supervisors and so engage them in the change process and give them adequate training for their new role.

3. EMPLOYEE INFORMATION

For staff to feel empowered, they must be informed. David Nadler of Delta Consulting noted in *Fortune* magazine (1992) 'In the organization of the future, information technology will be a load-bearing material – as hierarchy is now. Let information flow wherever it's needed, and the horizontal self-managed company is not only possible. It's inevitable.'

This approach is not prevalent in many traditional organizations in the UK. The journal *Industrial Society* (Webb, 1989) in its June 1988 MORI survey of persons employed in private sector companies found that most employees believed that they were at least fairly well informed, although only 19 per cent said that they were fully informed. Three out of four employees said that they could usually believe the information they were given. They were not very interested in financial information – only 39 per cent wanted to know about their company's financial performance and 27 per cent about the performance of the part of the company they worked for. Most employees wanted explanation rather than data and about matters that they saw as directly affecting them; 66 per cent wanted information on company plans for the future and 61 per cent said they would like to know how they are performing in their jobs. There was a surprisingly low interest in information about the company's products or services (35 per cent interested). The manual grade supervisors were nearly as interested as the management in quality information (51: 52 per cent).

These findings are to be expected in organizations where employees are not empowered. They are not involved in decision making and therefore they cannot put the information to practical use. Once employees are empowered they need access to information on all the chief parameters regarding the organization's performance so that they can contribute to the decisions that immediately affect them, and understand the decisions made by other teams.

Terry Walker, in his article 'Creating Total Quality Improvement that Lasts' (1992), states that quality programmes that work focus on educating people about the business and inspiring employees to help formulate essential goals and participate in the design and execution of strategies to deliver results. Ault, a dairy foods operation in North America, has spent the past five years focusing the attention of its workforce on understanding business results and the challenges of the market. The outcome has been impressive. Ault now runs the most efficient and profitable dairy foods operation in North America and in a unionized environment. See the checklist for management action at the end of this chapter to review your current communication and information systems.

4. APPROPRIATE TRAINING

Empowerment requires a total training programme starting from top management down to the front-line worker. Training is vital to support and enhance the organization's vision, mission and goals. Again one must check the reality of the organization and it may be necessary to make good the education deficits. For instance, Motorola found that its employees were intelligent and capable, but had inadequate skills, e.g. less than half of its front-line workers could pass a test with questions such as 'Ten is what per cent of 100?' In addition, employees with college degrees often lack college level skills. Motorola responded by establishing a programme to raise employee learning to the levels needed for a total quality work organization (Marshall and Tueber, 1992).

The Tennessee Eastman Company used training to move it from a culture of suggestion involvement through to the high involvement culture of interlocking teams. They implemented a multi-faceted improvement programme to support its push toward world-class performance. Each of the company's 7,800 employees spend about 80 hours in training. (J.H. Sheridan (1991), 'America's Best Plants: Tennessee Eastman', *Industry Week*, October, pp. 59–80.)

Training cannot be done on the cheap and should be viewed as an investment. Therefore treat training in the same way as any other investment, i.e. it must produce a measurable return. For example, a new cooperation between organized labour and management has been carried to lengths seldom seen before at General Motors. At each managerial level from the president down and within each staff function a union counterpart shares decision making equally with Saturn Division managers. The team is the basic organizational building block at Saturn. On the production floor, workers are grouped into teams of eight to 15 people. Each team has an elected leader called a work team counsellor. Above that level are groups of people called work unit module advisors, who serve as counsellors and troubleshooters for all work teams.

The whole system is supported by enormous amounts of training. Each new employee at Saturn goes through a week of orientation training before they start work. After this, they work only part time for the first two to three months as they split time between classroom and 'on the job' training. Production workers can expect to spend half their training time learning 'soft skills', such as conflict resolution, presentation skills, etc. Saturn's faith in the power of training is so resolute that it tied training to the company's 'risk and reward' compensation system. Each employee must commit to receiving at least 92 hours of training a year – about 5 per cent of total work hours, i.e. the company guarantees 95 per cent of their base wages and does not pay the remaining 5 per cent unless everybody meets the training goal. The first quarter goal was 155,687 hours: Saturn employees logged more than 300,000.

All this paid off. In 1991, Saturn sold more cars per dealer than any other manufacturer, including Honda, which had been the market leader for the previous two years (Geber 1992).

5. COMPATIBLE ORGANIZATIONAL SYSTEMS

Saturn's experience with training demonstrates that changing the structure of an organization into teams alone is not enough. All other organizational systems including job design, compensation, performance measures and employee relations must also be compatible and support the motivation and involvement of staff.

Professor Rosabeth Moss Kanter of Harvard Business School, in her address at the 1992 national conference of the Institute of Personnel Development, points out that in organizations that consist of teams, project groups and taskforces rather than department empires, 'People used to work to get a title, now they work to achieve a result. Rewarding people for their contribution frees them from the need to get promoted in order to get more money' (Golzen, 1992).

When Rover introduced its new deal aimed at securing long-term growth and prosperity through a new partnership with the company's employees and suppliers, as well as changing the way people worked, other organizational systems had to be changed as well. John Towers, Group Managing Director Rover, stated:

○   Rover will be a single status company. All distinctions between 'staff' and 'hourly paid' will be ended.
○   Continuous improvement will be a formal objective for every employee.
○   Employees will be required to be flexible in the work they undertake and to facilitate this flexibility the company will provide unrestricted access to tools, equipment and appropriate training.
○   There will be maximum devolution of authority and accountability to the employees actually doing the job.
○   Productivity bonus schemes will be focused on factors directly related to the performance of the company.
○   Constant, open and honest two-way communications will be the norm.

Rover felt that the only way it could be successful in the coming decade would be 'to attract, retain and motivate our employees to use our considerable talents in the interest of the firm' (Towers 1992).

PITFALLS TO AVOID

1.   Power conscious managers dislike empowerment. There is no doubt that the fundamental principle of empowerment is radically different from the traditional Western one of command and control as opposed to support and facilitate.
2.   Staff do not receive the support they need:
    ○   Goals are not clear.
    ○   Systems, processes and structures are inadequate.
    ○   Managers abdicate responsibility rather than facilitate and enable.
    ○   Staff are not trained in the skills they need to proceed.
3.   Democratic, involving methods are alien to people accustomed to the more authoritarian methods of the past. Some people do not like working this way and prefer the traditional way. Therefore you need to be patient and supportive and allow people time to adjust.
4.   Since there is no one design that fits every workplace, each organization creates its own version. Reassuring people when you do not have all the answers is a very difficult leadership task and requires an act of faith on the part of the leader.
5.   Since this new way requires much training and support, a difficulty can be moving too fast, before the necessary skills are learned.
6.   In a union environment extremely close cooperation is required. Managers and union leaders must become partners in improving staff motivation and involvement and this can only happen by letting go of traditional definitions, and redefining what is possible in a win-win relationship.

7.   Additional skills and knowledge are needed so much time and money must be invested in training costs.

8.   There is a danger that staff become empowered to make significant improvements but these may not be the highest priority from a customer point of view.

CHECKLIST FOR MANAGEMENT ACTION

HOW TO INTRODUCE A PROGRAMME FOR STAFF MOTIVATION AND INVOLVEMENT (based on Webb 1989)

1. Show commitment from the top.
    - ○ Chief executive personally committed to involving employers and reinforcing through their own behaviour.
    - ○ Board agrees the board objectives for employee involvement and ensures that all directors and managers have personal objectives that encompass employee involvement.
    - ○ Ensure that a strong effective communication strategy exists.
2. Make one person responsible for the implementation of employee involvement.
    - ○ Set up a steering group, including a senior manager who reports direct to the chief executive.
    - ○ Appoint a coordinator with a clear role and authority.
    - ○ Set up work/project groups to work with the coordinator.
3. Appraise the present situation.
    - ○ Carry out an audit and staff survey to identify the problems people see.
    - ○ Look at all the organizational systems, policies, procedures, decision making, recruitment policy and reward strategy to see if these support employee involvement.
4. Involve every level of management.
    - ○ In the design and process for involving employees.
    - ○ How it will be implemented in their area.
    - ○ Clarify their roles and the support they will have.
5. Involve recognized trade unions
    - ○ Effect on existing procedures for consultation and negotiation.
    - ○ How issues such as job design, teamworking, etc. are to be consulted on and discussed.
6. Agree a timetable for employee involvement.
    - ○ Agree what objectives, e.g. teamworking, job redesign, etc. are to be implemented and in what time scale.
    - ○ Provide for progress to be regularly monitored and reviewed.
7. Consult before decisions are made.
    - ○ Look at how the organization makes decisions.
    - ○ Ensure that the decision making system builds in consultation.
    - ○ Ensure that procedures for consultation are correctly followed.
    - ○ Develop and publicize a procedure for ensuring local issues are dealt with promptly at the appropriate level.
8. Look at the potential for delegating decisions.
    - ○ Decide what decisions can be delegated to individual teams.
    - ○ Train in teamworking and problem solving techniques.
    - ○ Provide teams with clear parameters within which to operate.

○ Ensure that teams are provided with the necessary information and resources.

9.   Look at job design and organizational structure.

○ Explore whether jobs can be restructured to improve motivation and performance.

○ Multi-skilling and delayering should be considered as options. These are explained in detail in Chapter 10.

10.   Communications.

○ Review your current communication systems.

○ Do you have newsletters, teambriefing, cascade systems, top-down managerial briefings, etc?

○ Do you communicate everything, including performance information, to staff?

○ How often are staff communicated with:
a)   formally;
b)   informally.

○ What involvement do staff really have in decision making, e.g. through self-managed teams, suggestion schemes, etc?

○ Can they tangibly see the results of this involvement?

○ How many significant decisions have been changed or adapted in the last year as a result of staff input?

○ How do staff feel about communication systems? Use staff surveys to assess how empowered staff feel in terms of:
a)   understanding the challenges before them;
b)   their ability to contribute to decisions with regard to these; and
c)   their role in meeting the challenges.

To communicate organizational objectives:

○ Involve as many people as possible in planning the future direction.

○ Communicate the objectives.

○ Ensure people understand and 'sign up' to them.

○ Ensure that employees understand the role of, and implications for, their work unit.

○ Constantly reinforce the objectives.

11.   Invest in training.

All training must be geared to developing the competencies required by the staff to deliver the business objectives and sustain the values of the organization. Assess the skills needed for employee involvement and ensure that all managers and employees are competent in these. The following procedure should therefore be followed:

○ Identify competencies required to deliver the business objectives in the three main areas:
a)   professional/technical;
b)   core; and
c)   managerial.

○ Develop and implement a process that enables people to assess themselves or be assessed against these required competencies.

○ Produce personal development plans for all members of staff.

○ Enable staff to achieve their personal development plan objectives by identifying with them training and development options.   ·

12. Get feedback.

○ Conduct regular surveys of employee attitudes and opinions.

○ Ensure that everyone knows what is really going on.

13. Share the benefits.

○ Review your reward strategy for both pay and non pay elements. What could you do to support employee involvement?

○ Plan how managers, employees and representatives will be trained to achieve a relevant understanding of how the business works and its performance.

5

TOTAL QUALITY MANAGEMENT

It's a funny thing about life; if you refuse to accept
anything but the best, you very often get it.
W. Somerset Maugham

Doing common things uncommonly well.
Henry J. Heinz, founder, H.J. Heinz & Co.

WHAT IS TOTAL QUALITY MANAGEMENT?

Total quality management (TQM) is a culture where all staff are dedicated to meeting customer needs on a 'right first time' basis. They do this by measuring their team's performance against predetermined targets covering all processes, products and services. Suggesting and implementing improvements is another shared responsibility, and the term continuous quality improvement (CQI) is often used now instead of TQM. There is great stress on cooperation and learning. As with any major culture change, it will take several years before the full benefits are realized. TQM is an all-embracing philosophy. It is a never-ending quest rather than a destination. It is certainly not a 'one-off' initiative.

TQM caught the attention of British and American companies when they saw it as the key to the growing dominance of Japanese manufacturing. Ironically, the Japanese systematic approach to quality was inspired by an American, W. Edwards Deming. Feeling that his message had gone unheard in America, he introduced it to Japan after the Second World War. The Japanese were so impressed by his efforts that they have even named their quality award after him. Many years later these lessons are being applied in the West.

The first attempts to implement TQM in Britain and America in the early 1980s tended to focus on one aspect, namely quality circles. Workers met in groups to suggest how they could increase productivity. Most of these initiatives failed because the entire organization did not adopt a quality culture. Managers carried on as before and were quick to sacrifice quality for short-term cost pressures. In addition, supervisors and managers felt threatened by improvements suggested by their staff. It only took managers to ignore a few good ideas for staff to become discouraged. Many circles then became talking shops and lost credibility throughout the organization. However, as more customers voted with their credit cards for Japanese goods, British and American organizations revisited TQM.

TQM can be implemented in quite different ways. Functional TQM reviews performance within a department. Where several sections within a department undertake their own reviews, this is a sub-functional TQM. The benefit of this method is that those involved are likely to know and understand each other quite well. Process TQM crosses functional departments and reviews a whole activity such as sales to delivery. This method is harder to implement as staff will need time to get to know each other and their problems. However, it has a greater potential for achieving significant improvements in quality as functional barriers in themselves can be the root of many problems. This approach moves TQM much closer to re-engineering, which we will review in the next chapter.

It is highly probable that Japanese culture is more in tune with TQM than our own in that it emphasizes cooperation, teamworking and long-term goals. The Japanese even have a word, *kaizen*, for making frequent, small improvements, something we do not have in English. We are more individualistic and competitive in our attitudes and focus on short-term financial results. This means that we have to change more of our culture, before TQM can flourish. Nevertheless, some British and American companies have benefited greatly from TQM through dedicating themselves to long-term goals.

Some organizations have rejected TQM as they believe that they cannot afford to improve quality. They fail to realize that poor quality is even more costly, resulting in scrap, reworking and frequent checks on quality. The biggest cost is likely to be advertising to replace disgruntled customers who have turned to competitors in their droves.

TQM can be linked to other strategies for change such as empowerment. In some factories workers have the right to stop the production line if they identify problems. Just-in-time manufacturing, which reduces the cost of stocks, work in progress and unsold goods, has also been introduced with TQM. The objectives for TQM in manufacturing are to eliminate:

O   excess – making products with no certainty of sale as they are not sufficiently appealing to customers;
O   waste – any action which does not add value to the customer; and
O   unevenness – stockpiles of work in progress generated by poorly coordinated production.

Under TQM, poor quality is seen as the fault of bad systems rather than unsatisfactory individual performance. This has significant consequences for how staff are rewarded and sits ill with individual performance-related pay. Linking reward to organizational change is tackled in greater detail in Chapter 11. Quality is enhanced by all staff working together to improve systems. While TQM has its origins in manufacturing, it can be applied to any organization.

Under TQM routine inspection is eliminated as it becomes the responsibility of each worker. The emphasis is on getting it 'right first time' rather than rectifying faults. Process time is therefore saved as there is no need to wait for an inspection by someone else, an objective central to re-engineering, which will be covered in the next chapter. The emphasis on 'right first-time' also supports flatter organizational structures as the inspection role of the supervisor is redundant.

DEFINING QUALITY

The quality of a good or service can be assessed from different perspectives. Some organizations define quality in a very limited way, but there are real benefits to be gained from using a broader definition, as Ron Zemke (1993) has done in the example below of buying a new car:

○   **Transcendental:** quality is innate excellence; does it immediately give that quality impression? Did the car door close easily? Do the car seats feel luxurious when you sit in them?

○   **Product based:** quality has to do with differences in the quantity of some desired ingredient or attribute. The high quality product is harder or softer or creamier or stronger than the lower quality product. How good are the attributes? Is the engine economical on petrol?

○   **User based:** quality is about fitness for use – the capacity of a product or service to satisfy customers' expectations and preferences throughout the whole life of the product, i.e. product reliability. For the urban motorist, is it easy to park in small spaces?

○   **Manufacturing based:** quality is about conformance to requirements – the degree to which a product conforms to its specifications. How often is your product not up to specification? How many cars fail the final quality inspection?

○   **Value based:** the highest quality product is the one that gives customers the most for their money – the one that meets customers' needs for the lowest price. Is your product the best value for money? What is its likely resale value in three years time? How reliable has it been?

Dr Noriaki Kano and colleagues (1991) suggest that each facet of quality can be graded as follows:

○   Reverse (very poor) quality.
○   Indifferent (poor) quality.
○   Expected quality.
○   Satisfying quality.
○   Delightful quality.

Expected quality is what needs to be achieved if customers are not to complain. *Satisfying quality* meets customer expectations. *Delightful quality* goes beyond providing satisfaction and gives customers something they really value but did not anticipate. It is the latter that differentiates a product and may allow a premium to be charged for it.

Table 5.1 illustrates the rating of similar products from two different types of organization. 'A' is an introverted organization that concentrates on production while B is an extrovert organization that focuses on customer requirements. A

TABLE 5.1   MEASURING QUALITY

Factor	Quality Measure				
	Reverse (very poor)	Indifferent (poor)	Expected (on target)	Satisfying (good)	Delightful (outstanding)
Transcendental: what is the immediate feel?			AB		
User based: what do customers think?		A		B	
Product based: how good are the ingredients?			B	A	
Manufacturing based: is it up to spec?			B	A	
Value: does it give customers most for their money?			A	B	

quick glance at the table will show that neither approach is enough. Quality has to be targeted on customers' expectations so that they can be exceeded.

HOW GOOD IS YOUR QUALITY?

Turning to your organization, how good is your quality? Use Table 5.2 to help you assess the quality of one of your key products. If you have scored under 15 you clearly have some quality problems. The next section will help you to put some of these right.

IMPLEMENTING TQM

The steps you will need to take to implement TQM in your organization are explained below.

CUSTOMERS COME FIRST

Start with a strong customer focus, otherwise your organization could mis-direct its efforts on improving aspects that customers find unimportant. Some factors that can make a difference to customers may not even be appreciated, let alone addressed. Take the example of packaging that is difficult to open. If users attack the product with knives or scissors, they are lucky not to damage it, let alone themselves. No doubt, the designers and production staff thought their job was done when they specified robust packaging to keep their product in optimal

TABLE 5.2   MEASURING YOUR OWN QUALITY

Factor	Quality Measure				
	Reverse (very poor)	Indifferent (poor)	Expected (on target)	Satisfying (good)	Delightful (outstanding)
Transcendental: what is the immediate feel?					
User based: what do customers think?					
Product based: how good are the ingredients?					
Manufacturing based: is it up to spec?					
Value: does it give customers most for their money?					
Score					

condition. They have not thought through what all aspects of their product mean for the poor customer. Even if all fit customers can cope with the package, what about the growing number of elderly people? Does the manufacturer really want to exclude them and the younger disabled people? This point is equally valid for shops and offices visited by customers. Access to premises rarely takes into account the needs of this group of customers or people with young children. How does your organization obtain this type of feedback? Do you have panels of customers to review what they think of your organization? Do you carry out market research?

The needs of internal customers are easy to overlook. In-house computer software often fails to live up to their expectations. It is not surprising that some cynics classify programmers as either nerds, who do the wrong things very well or hippies who do the right thing badly! Quality means concentrating on improving things that customers appreciate, rather than what organizations think they might want. The important lesson is to do the *right* things right rather than just doing things right. What mechanisms do internal customers in your organization have for measuring quality? Do they lead to regular improvements?

TQM can greatly improve services. You can use it to reduce long queues and excessive waits for someone to answer the phone. It is amazing how many organizations appear merely to tolerate customers. Staff in the worst performing organizations give customers the impression that they are unwanted and that they hope they will go elsewhere to give them a break. On the other hand, empowered staff can do much to improve relationships with customers, as we saw in Chapter 4. How well do your staff treat your customers? This too could be covered by your research.

LEADERSHIP

A quality culture will grow only if it is carefully nurtured from the top. It is for each organization to devise its own quality policy and to define what it means by quality. Quality will obviously form a key part of the mission statement. TQM can be greatly supported by powerful role models of senior staff showing that they are willing to make personal sacrifices to improve quality. Leaders should demonstrate their commitment. An enterprising hospital chief executive gives patients his home phone number in case they want to make a complaint, sending powerful messages to both patients and staff about the importance of getting it right first time. TQM has to be genuinely owned by all staff; it cannot be imposed on a top-down basis. It requires employees and suppliers to believe in and practise putting quality first in all aspects of their work.

COMMUNICATIONS

Improving communication between divisions and departments and both up and down the organization is a vital element of TQM. Front-line staff may have to carry the can for problems caused elsewhere. They receive the customer complaints yet those closer to the source of the problem can be blissfully unaware; a perfect recipe for losing customers. Communication includes sharing commercially sensitive information with staff to help them do their job better. It will also begin to gain their trust.

CULTURE

If TQM is to succeed, you need to build a quality culture based on a range of mutually reinforcing beliefs and values. Improving cooperation is vital as one person's work impacts on another. Other behaviours you should encourage are the capacity to question, to learn and to change. Create an atmosphere of trust where staff are fairly treated by managers. Have you already removed arbitrary status distinctions such as separate canteens and reserved parking places for senior staff as a first step? If not, what is stopping you? Staff also need to feel secure, otherwise they will be unwilling to suggest improvements that may eliminate jobs. Therefore every effort should be made to avoid compulsory redundancies. Your staff should feel valued. When things go wrong, you should emphasize solving the problem, rather than using information on quality to seek someone to blame. New cultures take time to nurture. You need to be committed to TQM as a long-term strategy.

If you want to build a culture where staff really care for customers, you need to treat your staff well in the first place. This point was not appreciated when staff were sent on customer care courses some years ago. Staff were taught to be polite and smile, and they did – for a month. Then they remembered that they had nothing to smile about! Such situations develop in organizations that do not tell staff immediately why something has gone wrong. When a customer complains, staff feel embarrassed. Do not be surprised if they say, 'Don't ask me, no one tells us anything.' Another example is provided by a company that repairs washing machines. When customers asked how much a repair was likely to cost, they were given a top and bottom price. The customers obviously hoped that they would be charged the lower price. When this did not happen they took their resentment out on the service engineer. Try smiling when that has happened to you ten times in a week. The solution proved to be quite simple. The company introduced a standard price, regardless of the cost of the repair. The customers knew where they stood and were happier with the new arrangement. The engineers could give a better service as they had a lower 'hassle factor'. Financially, the company did not lose out as the standard price was an average of the two prices.

MONITORING AND IMPROVING QUALITY

With TQM, each member of staff will become responsible for the quality of their own work. Routine inspection is eliminated as it becomes the responsibility of each worker and flatter organizational structures are developed as the inspection role of the supervisor is redundant. Empowerment in a service role is vital if staff are to take the initiative in exceeding customer expectations. They will have to be given greater discretion in solving problems and spending money. Many of the lessons from Chapter 4 on empowerment need to be applied if TQM is to succeed.

In addition to individuals becoming their own quality supervisor, work teams could regularly review their progress and tackle wider issues. You would almost certainly benefit from also having project teams that address issues that cross functional boundaries. For instance, quality should be built into products and services in the design and development phase as part of a process TQM project. Design and development should take into account consumer needs while also designing products that are easy to manufacture and assemble. Therefore, a designer's customers include all those who handle the product at any point.

Staff can gain a greater sense of ownership of TQM through quality improvement teams. Ideally, such teams should be drawn from staff representing every section and department that deal with a particular process. One way to avoid the group being taken over by dominant personalities is to ask them to write down their ideas. Each team member is given a pile of blank cards onto which they write one idea only. The first question might be 'why are deadlines missed?' After ten minutes or so the cards are pinned up on a board in groups. They might, for instance, refer to training or the lack of it, management, coordination and communication, etc. The next task is to see whether these problem areas are causally linked and need to be resolved in a particular sequence. The group can then be issued with more blank cards to come up with solutions.

In Chapter 2 we examined the difference between superficial change, which is of little benefit, and fundamental change, which radically improves performance, i.e. first and second order change, respectively. The way to achieve radical, second order change is by asking the question 'why?' Asking five times gets to the heart of matter as this example from Peter Scholtes (1993) shows:

O   Why is there oil on the floor? Because the machine is dripping oil.
O   Why is the machine dripping oil? Because the gasket is leaking.
O   Why is the gasket leaking? Because it is made of inferior material.
O   Why do we use gaskets of inferior material? Because the purchasing agent got a good deal on them.
O   Why is it important for the purchasing agent to get a good deal on gaskets? Because his performance is evaluated on how often he can get good deals.

One well-established TQM technique is for staff to work through a continuous cycle of planning, doing, checking and acting on the results so that quality is improved sometimes called the Deming cycle.

STAGED QUALITY CHECKS

Given the importance of the customer for TQM, it is with customer requirements that you should start your quality checks. These will tell you whether you have been concentrating on the key aspects of your product or service from the customer's point of view. You might also find out how best to develop the product. Quality checks can be made through discussion groups and surveys as already noted. The more imaginative organizations send staff to their customers to gain a better understanding of customer needs. This method also reinforces the importance of customers in the minds of staff.

The next stage in the quality cycle is when goods leave your premises. Only a sample of products is checked as separately checking every product is inconsistent with TQM, as we have seen. Quality checks during the production phase should be integral to the job of everyone involved. Systems should be in place that make it difficult for staff to make mistakes. There is a range of monitoring and diagnostic tools that can be used in this process, which will be covered later in this chapter. In manufacturing, quality checks should start at your suppliers. Not only should their products be of the required quality, their design needs to reflect your requirements as closely as possible. The importance of improving this relationship is explored in Chapter 9.

The first stage of customer requirements should influence all subsequent stages. When it comes to designing new products, design teams drawn from staff involved in the different stages of the cycle should be involved so that all phases are carefully integrated. This system will help to reduce cost by designing out unnecessary aspects that do not add value to the customer, and will ensure that quality is built into the product at each stage.

TQM uses a wide range of statistical techniques to measure quality. Your staff will be taught how to carry out their own measurements so that they have a greater sense of ownership. The objective is to set rigorous performance limits that are regularly monitored. Attention is placed on those defects that cause most of the problems. Pareto's law that 80 per cent of problems can be explained by 20 per cent of causes often applies.

ASSIGNING PRIORITIES

To ensure that your approach to TQM is focused, list all your projects and then rank them according to the column headings in Table 5.3. These headings are not mutually exclusive as benefits to customers could reflect lower costs and improved quality. However, having three separate headings places greater stress on each of these significant factors. Rank the projects by giving 1 for your first choice and so on. Deciding between projects is very much a matter of personal judgement. We have selected Project B as our first choice overall as a quick win to build up confidence; it will take only two months to complete and is ranked second under 'Probability of success'. It is also our second choice under 'Benefits to customers'. The most popular project from the customer perspective is Project C, but this would take 18 months to implement and would have a lower probability of success. Therefore it is ranked only second overall. You could involve your project teams in the assessment and then summarize the results. This involvement will build up their sense of commitment.

The case study overleaf reveals the impressive results that can come from a strong commitment to TQM. It shows that success depends not on one factor, but on the whole range. These factors can be summarized as the 5 c's, namely:

O   **Customer** needs are the centre of all business activity.
O   A **culture** of quality is actively pursued throughout the organization and by suppliers.
O   **Commitment** and demonstration that quality comes first, from the top and through investing in training for all.
O   **Communication** about quality and customer needs flows continuously across departmental and functional boundaries.
O   A **count** is made of instances when performance falls below target.

TABLE 5.3   ASSIGNING PRIORITIES BETWEEN PROJECTS

Project	Benefit to customers	Cost saving	Improved quality	Speed to implement	Probability success	Ranking
A	5	1 (£250k)	4	=3 (9 months)	1	4
B	2	4 (£100k)	3	1 (2 months)	2	1
C	1	2 (£200k)	2	5 (18 months)	3	2
D	3	3 (£150k)	1	=3 (9 months)	5	3
E	4	5 (£50k)	5	2 (3 months)	4	5

Case study: Quality – Design to Distribution

Design to Distribution Ltd (D2D), a subsidiary of ICL specializing in contract electronics, won the European Quality Award in 1994. It has a turnover of £290 million and employes 2000 staff. It faces tough competition from the Far East.

D2D came top for overall customer satisfaction, hardware reliability and quality of installation, as measured twice yearly by an independent organization. Its turnaround times are very fast. It supplies PCs in a day, which matches its best performing competitor, and is 25 per cent quicker than its nearest rival in supplying customized mainframes. Examples of poor quality are extremely rare. Only 0.3 per cent of consignments were incorrect and it had fewer than 3 failures per million for 40 per cent of its processes. Profits have increased by 50 per cent in the two years since D2D became independent. Revenue per employee is 20 per cent higher than its closest competitor.

These achievements reflect D2D's aims to improve efficiency continuously, to reduce costs and defects and to provide better value to customers. It used sophisticated benchmarking to measure its performance internally, against ICL as well as with its customers, suppliers and competitors. Its key focus is customer satisfaction. It spends a great deal of effort in developing relationships with customers.

Each year the managing director, Alastair Kelly, talks to small groups of staff at all levels on quality issues. Training is taken very seriously and 5 per cent of payroll costs is spent on it. All managers are trained in quality education, awareness and quality improvement for the individual as well as customer care. Staff are given audiotapes covering key policies and objectives.

Quality circles and corrective action teams meet once a week. Rank Xerox, a previous European Quality Award winner, contributed to an empowerment workshop. All staff attended workshops on team effectiveness. D2D made a special point of making awards to over 500 individuals who had made noteworthy contributions to quality. Employee surveys showed that 70 per cent of staff felt that they were encouraged to participate in cross boundary teams. A greater percentage felt that their cooperation in their own team had improved. Operators can stop production to prevent quality falling below prescribed standards. Unplanned staff turnover is very low for the industry at only 2 per cent.

Quality initiatives are now used by D2D to bring about strategic improvements such as reducing time to market. Tracking work in progress has also been simplified and improved by introducing a better IT system.

Source: Summarized from *UK Quality*, March 1995, pp. 20–5

A TQM ACTION PLAN

Deming (1986) produced a 14-step plan that has been used by many organizations. The steps are as follows:

1. **Create purpose constantly for the organization**. The provision of quality goods and services is the number one priority. Profits will come as a by-product of TQM rather than being the primary objective.

2. **Adopt and understand the never-ending improvement philosophy**. The TQM philosophy needs to be actively pursued by all staff and must be seen as a long-term commitment.

3. **Replace mass inspection with statistical monitoring of the never-ending improvement of the production process**. Managers who check the work of their staff reduce their sense of responsibility and ownership. If staff take pride in quality and are fully supported in this aim, inspection is unnecessary.

4. **Change the philosophy of awarding business on the basis of price**. Supplier relationships based on long-term cooperation can result in components and services from suppliers being tailored much more closely to the needs of their customers. This is explored in Chapter 9.

5. **Strive constantly to improve the system rather than blame workers for the company's problems**. Most problems are caused by the way work is organized, which tends to thwart staff who want to work well.

6. **Institute modern methods for training workers**. Most of the effort and money put into training tends to be concentrated on the higher and middle echelons of organizations. Workers need to be trained in how to do their jobs better and how to use the TQM monitoring tools.

7. **Focus more on supervisors providing a supportive environment of workers**. Supervisors should act as coaches and trainers as they no longer have an inspection role.

8. **Drive out fear that employees may have about telling management about problems**. Supervisors and managers should not punish staff who challenge the way work is carried out. In fact, constructive discussion should be encouraged.

9. **Break down the organizational barriers that exist in today's businesses**. Organizations that still have separate canteens and reserved parking spaces are sending signals to those outside the sacred circle that they are second best.

10. **Eliminate arbitrary numerical goals and integrate personal goals with the organization's overall goal of never-ending improvement of quality**. Empowered staff who feel valued and trusted will be more prepared to sign up to this goal than those directed to do so.

11. **Replace management by numbers with statistical methods for measuring never-ending quality improvement**. Placing the emphasis on production quotas means that staff will not treat quality as the top priority.

12.   **Facilitate and promote pride of workmanship**. Staff need to be given good quality materials, equipment and working conditions. The underlying assumption is that staff are doing their best, which means that individual appraisal systems will undermine their morale and commitment.

13.   **Institute extensive education and training at every level of the organization**. The emphasis here is on team building and other behaviours that support TQM.

14.   **Structure the organization so that all staff are involved in never-ending quality improvement.** Management leadership and commitment to change, along with an implementation strategy, are essential.

EVALUATION AND ACCREDITATION

Even if you do not want to apply for the British Quality Foundation's UK Quality Award or obtain the British Standard for quality, you can still gain from adapting some of the measures and approaches that these bodies recommend.

THE UK QUALITY AWARD

The annual Quality Award, presented by the British Quality Foundation, has attracted many leading organizations from a wide range of sectors. It encourages organizations to assess themselves against agreed criteria. The marks are equally divided between enabling factors and results. This approach involves satisfying the expectations of a wide range of stakeholders and puts customers before shareholders, which may come as a surprise to some companies. Healthy organizations, however, realize that they have a future only if they make customers their first priority. The key stakeholders are ranked as follows: customers (customer satisfaction – 20 per cent); shareholders (business results – 15 per cent); staff (people satisfaction – 9 per cent); the community and beyond (impact on society – 6 per cent). Some narrowly focused organizations may find the last factor unexpected but forward thinking organizations realize that they have to be in accord with the local population where they carry out their business. If they fail to do so, they might find themselves on the receiving end of a boycott as Shell did in Germany over its plan to dump a redundant oil rig in the North Sea. Figure 5.1 shows the allocation of marks in greater detail.

Will this approach help your organization? It will give you the following advantages:

O   It is a comprehensive and structured approach and includes many of the aspects of TQM that we have covered above.

O   You can compare your progress over time as the approach provides benchmarks.

O   You can compare your organization with many others throughout Europe.

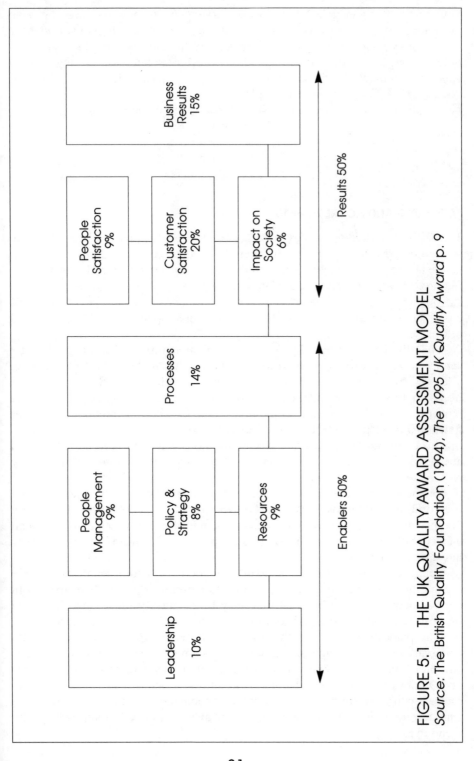

FIGURE 5.1   THE UK QUALITY AWARD ASSESSMENT MODEL
Source: The British Quality Foundation (1994), *The 1995 UK Quality Award* p. 9

You should consider going through the self-assessment process once you have made a real step forward with your quality campaign, as it will help you identify what more you could achieve. The attraction of the Quality Award is that it also reflects outcomes, in contrast to the British Standard for quality, which concentrates more on whether you have robust processes in place, than what you actually achieve in the market-place.

For further information contact: The British Quality Foundation
215 Vauxhall Bridge Road
London SW1V 1EN
Tel. 0171-963 8000
Fax. 0171-963 8001

STANDARDS AND ACCREDITATION

The British Standard for quality is BS EN ISO 9000, which has replaced BS 5750. It requires organizations to follow carefully documented procedures, setting out in detail the responsibilities and structures that affect quality. Management is required to review performance on a regular basis. This should be supported by quality audits that assess the system's effectiveness and an analysis of customer complaints. (The importance of linking suppliers into TQM is covered in Chapter 7.)

While the BS was originally devised for manufacturing, it can be used in the service sector. It is being revised to address specifically the needs of marketing, sales and customer service functions. The revisions will cover reflecting customer needs in business and marketing plans; how to make best use of customer information; and improving communications between marketing and other functions. In response to previous criticisms the accreditation process for small organizations has been streamlined. Organizations wanting to reach the Standard are advised to hire a TQM consultant to guide them through the many requirements.

For the organization to obtain real value, the working documents must be used and regularly updated. Manuals drawn up only to achieve accreditation are doomed to gather dust. For this reason, gaining the British Standard has been viewed by some more as an advertising ploy than a means of continuously improving quality.

Would gaining the British Standard be good for your organization? Some organizations see it as an advantage in the market-place as it sets them apart from the competition. The risk is that they may lose sight of the fact that the prime purpose of quality initiatives is to improve quality and reduce costs. Instead they proudly paint their vans with the BS logo and believe that the job is done. BS also places a heavy emphasis on written documentation setting out standards and procedures. Make sure that your organization has experienced the benefits of TQM and that there are champions at all levels before you consider the BS route. If you are a supplier, some of your customers may put pressure on you to gain accreditation, particularly if they are heavily committed to improve quality themselves.

PROBLEMS AND HOW TO AVOID THEM

Two-thirds of American TQM programmes fail according to the *Wall Street Journal* (Caudron, 1993). One of the problems of poorly implemented TQM programmes is the loss of focus. TQM can run out of steam if you concentrate on improving too many different processes at once while not taking sufficient account of customer needs. Joseph Juran, one of the original advocates of TQM, stresses the need to find the 20 per cent of causes that generate 80 per cent of the problems (Pareto's law). However, to truly bring about significant improvements for customers the causes that need identifying should be those which bring the biggest return to them. You can avoid these risks by using Table 5.1 to help you prioritize your projects.

Organizations can take a too short-term perspective. They can underestimate the difficulty and the time required to change employee behaviour. It may be that the requisite changes are not forthcoming. By using the UK Quality model you will have benchmarks to monitor your progress and help you refocus your efforts. In addition you could increase the commitment and understanding of your staff by encouraging them to visit customers.

There is a danger that the lack of quick results can also lend to disenchantment with TQM. This problem can be exacerbated by emphasizing those TQM aspects that have a long-term payback such as culture building and benchmarking. One way around this problem is to implement improvements that make a breakthrough in organizational performance. You could do this by identifying the process or activity that would give you the best short-term return if it were improved. Examples might be speeding up new product development or reducing scrap rates. You could then give this task to a project manager and team to implement. This approach, along with ownership by top management and training the team in the use of diagnostic tools, moves TQM much closer to re-engineering. Team members agree a workplan with milestones, deliverables and reviews. You will have then built the foundation of a TQM programme that you can extend to the whole organization.

TQM stresses the importance of improving communication between departments and functions. This, while laudable in itself, may not be enough to make a real improvement. It may be that a process is unmanageable because it crosses too many departmental boundaries. You should consider restructuring the organization so that the process is under the control of one manager to whom all the staff involved report. This more radical approach lies at the heart of re-engineering, covered in the next chapter. In a step in this direction, TQM now places more emphasis on flow charts, which are an essential part of re-engineering.

Your reward strategy needs to be consistent with TQM. One such approach is competency-based pay covering the different aspects of the job, policies and product knowledge. Another is gainsharing, passing on some of the cost savings to staff, as covered in Chapter 11. Training is essential given the need to change attitudes and enhance competencies in measuring quality and teamworking. Globe Metallurgical, a North American company, gives each member of staff six hours of training in quality control techniques. The results are very impressive and every one dollar spent on quality produces a return of $40 (Elmuti *et al.* 1992). Your training programme should include team building, team leadership, communication skills, problem solving techniques and culture change.

You should seriously consider using process TQM to improve and speed up the design, development and introduction of new products. According to Insead Professor Arnoud de Meyer (1993), failure to do this is the reason why European manufacturing companies have neither improved profitability nor increased market share, despite improving quality, meeting delivery deadlines and improving reliability.

Table 5.4 will help you assess how much ground you might need to make up if you want to follow the TQM route. If you score 20 or more, then TQM could be very attractive as you have plenty to gain. A score between 15–19 would indicate a good case for TQM. A score of 10 or under means that you are aready experiencing the benefits of TQM, without perhaps knowing it!

TABLE 5.4   ASSESSING WHETHER TQM IS FOR YOUR ORGANIZATION

Factors	Rating				
	A great deal 5	Con- siderable 4	Moderate 3	Little 2	Very little 1
1. How much scope is there to improve quality to delight customers?					
2. How much scope is there to reduce costs by cutting our waste?					
3. How much can staff increase pride in their work?					
4. How much can cooperation between functions be improved?					
5. How much time have you got to make a big improvement?					
Total					

CHECKLIST FOR MANAGEMENT ACTION

1.   Assess customer requirements.
   O   Find our what your customers think through market research and customer focus groups.
   O   What is the quality of your services to internal customers?
2.   Provide leadership.
   O   What could your chief executive do to show that he or she believes in quality?
   O   Is quality adequately reflected in you mission statement?
   O   What could you and your colleagues do to show your commitment?
   O   How will you recruit more role models?
3.   Improve communications.
   O   What information, including commercially sensitive material, should you share with your staff?
   O   How are you going to communicate with staff on a regular basis, e.g. e-mail, newsletters?
4.   Develop and support a quality culture.
   O   How can you reduce the hassle factor of your staff?
   O   How will you become aware of staff who excel and how will you reward them?
   O   What do you and your colleagues need to do to prepare yourselves for a more articulate workforce?
5.   Monitor and improve quality.
   O   Over what period of time will you pass the responsibility for quality on to staff?
   O   What impact will this change have on the role of managers?
   O   Will you have scope to flatten your organizational structure?
   O   How can you bring design and production staff together to build in quality?
   O   Set up quality improvement groups. They should include some staff drawn from each aspect of a process as well as functional groups that could be a team or department.
   –   Use the 'ask why five times' technique.
   –   Use the high involvement technique using cards for each problem or issue.
   –   Teach the use of some of the tools and techniques that we will cover in Chapter 8.
6.   Carry out staged quality checks.
   O   Start reviewing quality at the stage goods or services are delivered to customers and then progress back down the chain.

6

RE-ENGINEERING

The impossible is often the untried
Jim Goodwin

The worst rule of management is 'If it ain't broke,
don't fix it.' In today's economy, if it ain't broke, you
might as well break it yourself, because it soon will
be.
Wayne Calloway, CEO, PepsiCo

R e-engineering aims to turn history on its head. Its authors, Michael
Hammer and James Champy, present it as a revolution. They argue that
we should reverse the strategy of the last two centuries of seeking to
achieve lower costs by breaking work into small tasks so that workers can
become more proficient. The division of labour was first put forward by Adam
Smith in *The Wealth of Nations*, published in 1776. He described how a pin
factory was much more productive because the work was broken into eighteen
distinct tasks, of which a worker would undertake only two or three.
Mechanization was encouraged by this simplification of tasks. A further big
reduction in costs and faster production came with the introduction of the
assembly line, popularized by Henry Ford.

The fragmented tasks, however, required a great deal of coordination.
Supervisors and quality controllers sought to get the most from a bored
workforce who repeated the same actions many times each hour. This way of
working was widely copied in factories and offices throughout the industrialized
world. It flourished in the post-war era that required long production lines to
meet the ever-growing demand from expanding markets. Customers were only
too pleased to become members of a consumer society through buying their
fridges, freezers and cars and at first they were satisfied with the narrow range
of models and variants that mass production could offer.

Mass production of this type flourished with the shortages after the Second
World War. It continued by meeting the demand from a more prosperous
working class and the new export markets. However, this approach was
threatened once markets became saturated. More goods become affected by the
dictates of fashion. Consumers demanded a wider range of products and services
that were much more closely geared to their needs. This favoured flexible,

extrovert, customer-focused organizations and led to the next change in organization design – just-in-time manufacturing.

JUST-IN-TIME PROCESSES

Just-in-time (JIT) manufacturing cuts costs by reducing stocks and work in progress. Goods are produced to meet customer orders. This avoids stockpiling products that may have to be sold at a discount due to lack of demand. Work in progress is reduced as stock piles at each stage of the process are massively reduced. The aim is to eliminate waste in the widest sense: anything that adds cost to production without adding value. Preventative maintenance is essential to support JIT to minimize the amount of down time due to machines breaking down.

JIT was pioneered by Toyota and became widespread in Japan in the 1970s. Western organizations began to introduce it towards the end of the decade in an attempt to emulate the Japanese achievements. Before JIT, many factories were optimized to make the most of their expensive capital equipment, rather than to achieve the most efficient use of staff. As a consequence, goods were moved substantial distances from one group of specialized machines to another. Coordination was difficult as many workers were involved. The large number of steps in the process increased both the number of potential bottlenecks and defects. However, cut-throat competition is forcing organizations to analyse their cost structures rigorously. Many have discovered that they can reduce their overall costs more by making the effective use of staff and the reduction of waste a higher priority than efficient use of machines. It is for each organization to calculate this balance for itself every few years. The answer could change as in some industries equipment costs have fallen in relation to labour costs in recent years.

Quality is improved because buffer stocks are usually eliminated, which means that any defective work is quickly exposed as it holds up the process. This encourages corrective action as the consequences of such hold ups are serious. With such a strong emphasis on quality it is no surprise that JIT is sometimes implemented as part of a TQM programme. It is a lengthy process to implement and seeks continuous improvement.

JIT requires good teamworking as workers can produce another unit only when the next work station indicates that it is needed. The most suitable form of organization is semi-autonomous teams of multi-skilled operatives. A more empowered workforce is another requirement. Teams in some organizations do their own recruiting. Training in diagnostic skills for problem solving often pays dividends. Fewer supervisors are required as staff take on many of their responsibilities. The remaining supervisors do more coaching, scheduling and planning. This transition can be too difficult for some. The reward strategy needs to reflect the emphasis of teamworking and quality (see Chapter 11).

The next step on is 'lean production', which uses fewer resources, still. Savings are made in the workforce, materials, time and space, following the example set by Toyota.

Case study: Introducing just-in-time processes – BICC plc

BICC plc was a traditional manufacturer that needed to change to survive. Bottlenecks were frequent, making it difficult to increase production. As a result of introducing JIT late orders were reduced from 1370 to 219. Scrap and absentee levels also declined.

Production was simplified by re-organizing around four cells of families of related products. All the machines required for a particular product family were grouped together. Staff became responsible for a total product rather than small parts of many different products. The staffing structure was changed to four teams, each with cell leaders reporting to a unit manager. This replaced the traditional structure of foreman, superintendent and unit manager.

A key feature of just-in-time processes is coordinating the volume of production at each stage. Where there is a bottleneck, staff involved elsewhere in the same process stop their own work and help overcome the problem. This quickly brings production back to speed and avoids the cost of creating stockpiles.

The company increased its investment in training and all staff went on team building courses. Staff flexibility was increased by training staff to work on any machine in the cell.

The old pay scheme encouraged operatives to work on machines that offered the highest bonuses, rather than to produce goods that were in demand. It also encouraged them to stockpile outputs when there were bottlenecks elsewhere. BICC introduced a single-status employment package and one pay spine, based on skill, for all employees below manager.

Source: Summarized from Keith Bott and Ron Johnson (1992), 'New Strands for Quality', *Personnel Management*, July, pp. 36–9

The main advantages of JIT are as follows:

O   Reducing waste – greater flexibility.
O   Quicker response to customer demand.
O   Shorter throughput times.
O   Lower stock levels.
O   Less work in progress.
O   Less space required due to lower stocks.
O   Fewer bottlenecks as they are immediately apparent and get sorted out.
O   Less down time due to component shortages.
O   Lower supervision costs.
O   Improved quality as feedback on problems is quicker.

DEMAND FLOW TECHNOLOGY

Demand flow technology takes JIT a step further in sophistication as it gears production even more closely to demand. The golden rule is that raw materials are pulled through only in response to demand. Gateway 2000, a cut price computer manufacturer, actually make machines to order. They do this by getting their customers to place their orders over the phone. They start to build their machine only after the customer's cheque has been cleared. This eliminates bad debts and gives Gateway a healthy cash flow as it receives its money before it has to pay its suppliers. The company is sufficiently quick in assembly and testing that it can supply the computer within a matter of days. In an industry where model life is measured in months rather than years, it avoids the cost of having to shift obsolete computers and components.

Demand flow technology combines all the benefits of batch production but with the lower costs of mass production. Parts are produced for the next worker only when they are needed. This Japanese approach, called *kanban*, further minimizes work in progress. To maximize flexibility, some tasks are less automated than in other plants. Large plants have more scope to make savings as they are less efficient because they are harder to manage.

High levels of efficiency depend on workers having more skills to a greater depth, for instance programming skills are important. Staff can move from work station to work station to cover variations in workload, and sickness and absence. Quality control is the responsibility of each worker. This places a premium on training, development and motivation.

Demand flow technology achieves lower costs through the following:

O   Lower stock levels.
O   Increased machine utilization.
O   Simpler stock control systems.
O   Lower set-up, waiting and moving times.
O   Reduced plant size.
O   Improved quality.
O   Multiskilled workers.

BUSINESS PROCESS RE-ENGINEERING

The next step in the development of organization design was the emergence of business process re-engineering, or what is now simply called re-engineering. It was first put forward by Michael Hammer in 1990 (Hammer, 1990) and has excited much enthusiasm. It has been defined as 'the fundamental rethinking and radical redesign of business processes to achieve dramatic improvements in critical, contemporary measures of performance, such as cost quality, service and speed' (Hammer and Champy, 1993, p. 32).

Re-engineering can turn introverted organizations into customer-oriented ones. It fundamentally questions the purpose of everything that is done. The first question is not how could a task be done better, but should it be done at all? How does it add value to the customer? Much work is actually done to meet the introverted needs of the organization rather than those of the customer. Re-engineering involves starting from scratch with a blank sheet of paper. It is a giant leap into a new world, rather than a few, tentative steps from the old. Companies such as First Direct can transform an industry by offering customers both greater convenience and lower costs. They achieve this by having very different and far superior processes. First Direct's phone banking service is built around the rapid retrieval and processing of client information by computer. This gives First Direct a competitive advantage over traditional banks in that it provides a 24 hour, seven days a week telephone banking service. This caters for busy people who are do not want to use banks in normal working hours. There are also cost savings for First Direct in that it does not have its own branch network with the associated staffing.

The most powerful tool of re-engineering is analysis and redesign of processes. A process has been defined as 'a set of linked activities that take an input and transform it to create an output' (Johansson et al. 1993, p. 57). Companies typically have 10 to 20 processes. Examples of important processes include design-to-production, prospect-to-sale, sale-to-delivery. They affect the way work is done and how machines and information and management technology are used. The objective of re-engineering is to make processes faster, simpler and more efficient. The outcome should aim also for higher quality by eliminating errors.

In successful re-engineering projects, process times are reduced from weeks to days. This is because most of them include plenty of idle time, with activity that adds value to customers representing only a fraction of the total. Delay and poor quality can result when a process is split between different departments or sections, which then become difficult to coordinate. Work is 'handed off' from one member of staff to the next. Customer needs may be overlooked as staff can have mutually inconsistent priorities and objectives. Even if staff meet all their targets the customer may still lose out.

Over time, processes can become overelaborate to enable them to cope with rare, complex problems. The most convoluted processes tend to be those designed to meet all eventualities. This means that many simple cases take much longer than necessary and are far costlier to process. This can happen when the cross-checks and supervision for high risks spread to low risk activities. An example of this was the move away from home births to hospital births to protect the vulnerable mother and child. However, many perfectly healthy mothers resented being in hospital. The NHS now appreciates that low risk births can take place at home, whereas high risk births should take place in hospital.

Quality can also be improved by simplifying processes. The fewer steps in the process chain and the fewer people involved, the smaller the scope for errors and bottlenecks. Less time and effort need to be spent on coordination. This means eliminating as many 'hand-offs' as possible. A re-engineered process has relatively self-contained teams with more specialist competencies. These were formerly located in central departments, which can now be reduced in size.

Case study: Re-engineering health care – patient focused care

A study of the Lakeland Regional Medical Centre, Florida by Booz Allen & Hamilton showed how incredibly complex and hard to manage hospitals can be. The 2300 employees worked in 70 departments and belonged to nearly 400 job classifications, three-quarters of which had less than 10 employees.

A routine X-ray took 40 steps, 140 minutes of staff time and involved 15 to 20 employees. Only 15 per cent of time was devoted to medical and clinical activities, the remaining 85 per cent was taken up by moving the patient, communication, coordination and clerical work. The same problem affected laboratory tests. They were often too late to be of use or had to be repeated due to over-complicated processes.

How work is organized can have a much bigger impact on costs than changing who does what to improve efficiency. In a traditional hospital, activities are concentrated in central departments and patients are moved from department to department. The huge number of steps and staff involved mean that staff spend more time in down time, waiting for patients, coordinating activity and clerical work than they do treating patients. A separate study in England by Andersen Consulting found that the average junior doctor walks about seven miles a day on duty, which takes two to three hours. This research showed that the average patient meets 47 different members of staff in a five-day hospital stay.

The solution is to move most activities nearer the patient, which means decentralizing as much as possible. The constraints are where very expensive equipment or highly specialized skills are involved. The hospital is divided into mini-hospitals with 75 to 125 beds, which provide over 90 per cent of care for their patients. The location of patients is heavily influenced by their use of resources. This may involve mixing patients together who would traditionally be kept separate, such as in-patients and out-patients. Staff are trained to have a wider range of skills and to work in teams.

The continuity of care is improved as fewer staff are in contact with the patient. The quality of care is better as nurses spend more time looking after patients, rather than on clerical tasks, and less time is wasted waiting for test results.

Sources: John Smith, Senior Vice President, Booz Allen & Hamilton (1989), 'The Patient Focused Hospital', The Twenty-sixth International Hospital Congress, The Hague, Netherlands, 31 May; Andersen Consulting (1993) *Patient Centred Care.*

Re-engineering draws on a large body of knowledge. There are some similarities with JIT such as simplifying processes, reducing the number of separate tasks undertaken by different workers and the emphasis on multi-skilling. However, JIT is specially geared to the factory environment while any organization can be re-engineered.

The six principles of re-engineering according to Hammer are as follows:

O   To organize around outcomes not tasks.
O   To have those who use the output of the process perform the process.
O   To subsume information processing work into real work that produces information.
O   To treat geographically dispersed resources as though they were centralized.
O   To put the decision point where the work is performed, and build control into the process.

Business process re-engineering can be subdivided between process re-engineering and business re-engineering. Process re-engineering has the more limited objective of focusing on a particular process, such as product development. This approach may be attractive to a successful organization seeking to get better still. Business re-engineering involves changing the whole organization. This approach may appeal to organizations under severe threat or highly ambitious, successful organizations. You need to assess your likely level of support and the risks and benefits of each approach.

Hammer and Champy argue that re-engineering is a top-down process because staff are unwilling to bring about radical changes that may result in job losses. This is reflected in their cycle of change which is as follows:

O   Re-engineer business process.
O   Change jobs and structures.
O   Change management systems.
O   Values and beliefs change as a result.

However, in the Thorn EMI case study in Chapter 2, it is clear that you can actually start by changing peoples' beliefs so that they support re-engineering. Therefore, you have a choice of how you wish to proceed.

HOW TO RE-ENGINEER

The following steps are based on the hard-won experience of numerous successful and unsuccessful re-engineering projects. You may wish to adapt them to meet the needs of your own organization.

ENERGIZE

The vital starting points of gaining commitment and creating a vision have been covered in Chapters 2 and 3. The commitment of your chief executive is crucial, as is the appointment of a full-time project manager with direct reporting lines. The next step is to set demanding goals such as to reduce a ten-week process to four days. If not, incremental change will creep in as staff will prefer to cling to existing practices. The objective is to be not just slightly better than the competition, but to move into another league.

You need to ensure that there is someone who is wholly committed to championing improvements to a specific process. You can achieve this by appointing a process owner to play a key role in all the phases of design, implementation, and maintaining and improving the process over the longer term.

You may not gain widespread support for change due to fears of job cuts and lost promotional opportunities that may result from re-engineering. You could lessen these fears by assessing the scope for reducing jobs without making compulsory redundancies. For instance, how many staff are likely to leave through voluntary wastage? Would a recruitment freeze and the use of temporary staff create the necessary headroom? How many staff are eligible for early retirement? How attractive is the voluntary redundancy package? Finally, what is the scope for redeployment and retraining?

The most frequent regret of organizations undertaking substantial change is that they wish they had communicated more with all their stakeholders. Therefore you need a strategy that maximizes the flow of information up and down your organization. Use as may media and approaches as possible. Communication is more than broadcasting your message; it includes listening and responding to the criticism and anxiety of your staff.

PRIORITIZE: SELECT A PROCESS TO RE-ENGINEER

Processes that are carried out frequently with a fair degree of consistency are good candidates for re-engineering. It may not be cost effective or even useful for you to re-engineer processes carried out infrequently, or those which require very variable responses. It is important that you select a process to re-engineer which will give large customer benefits. You can highlight where to concentrate your efforts, collect information on cost, quality, service and time, and the relative value customers put on each of them. Where your products are facing shorter product lives you might choose to focus on improving their design-to-production process. Most important of all is to start with a process which will give you a quick win. This will increase staff confidence in tackling more demanding processes. Beginning with a project with long lead times will play into the hands of the cynics. They will say that 'because nothing has happened yet, nothing ever will. It's just like all the other failed initiatives tried around here.'

The objective is to have products that are not just slightly better than those of the competition, but are obviously superior. You can achieve this by searching for breakpoints. Johansson *et al.* (1993, pp. 116–19) have categorized the following breakpoints:

○ **Robustness** – fitness for use by customers and ease of manufacture or supply.

○ **Price**.

○ **Lead time** – the time between receiving and fulfilling an order; the time taken to obtain parts. This can be reduced by empowering staff to make decisions themselves without seeking higher authority. Reductions in the amount of checking and supervision will lead to further improvements. Incorporate the competencies required for a process that were previously in separate functions.

○ **Flexibility** – the capacity to respond to different customer requirements; very important in manufacturing where machine reset time can be significant. Multi-skilled staff are necessary.

○ **Process design** – the simplest, most effective means of meeting customer needs.

○ **Service empathy** – a positive attitude to customers by all staff.

○ **Reliability** – the degree of certainty components will arrive just-in-time. Work closely with suppliers to achieve improvements. Resist the temptation to dump problems on suppliers, rather work with them to solve problems jointly in a creative partnership.

○ **Differentiation/optionality** – special product features that mark you out from the competition.

○ **Product design** – design products which are cheap and easy to manufacture. Close relationships between designers, production engineers and suppliers are needed.

○ **Information systems** – use information management and technology (IM&T) to reduce the time spent on collecting and processing data. Reduce duplication by sharing information with suppliers and customers.

○ **Environmental proactivity** – getting a step ahead in environmental responsibility, e.g. Sainsbury pays its customers 1p for every carrier bag they reuse. This may divert attention from actions that are not supportive of the environment such as encouraging greater use of cars by siting new stores outside towns away from public transport.

Now you are in position to apply this information to your own organization by completing Table 6.1. Scores of 'poor' and 'very poor' point the way.

ANALYSE

It is very illuminating literally to walk through the process to see who does what and why. You can ask staff why they are filling in a particular form and with whom they have to communicate to get things done. You can obtain a detailed understanding by mapping the existing system. This analysis will expose problems and bottlenecks and point to where improvements can be made both immediately and in the future. Figure 6.1 shows how this can be done. A more detailed example is provided in Chapter 8.

TABLE 6.1   FINDING YOUR ORGANIZATION'S BREAKPOINT FOR RE-ENGINEERING

Factor	Score				
	V. good 5	Good 4	Aver- age 3	Poor 2	V. poor 1
Robustness How fit is your product or service for customer needs?					
Price How do you compare on price?					
Lead time How does yours compare with your competitors?					
Flexibility How easily and quickly can you respond to changing customer needs?					
Process design How efficient and effective are your processes?					
Service empathy Do your staff treat customers really well?					
Differentiation How special are your products or services?					
Reliability Do you minimize costs through just-in-time deliveries from very dependable suppliers?					
Product design How cheap and easy are your products to manufacture or services to deliver?					
Information systems How well does IM&T support your organization?					
Environmental proactivity How well would your organization score in a green audit?					

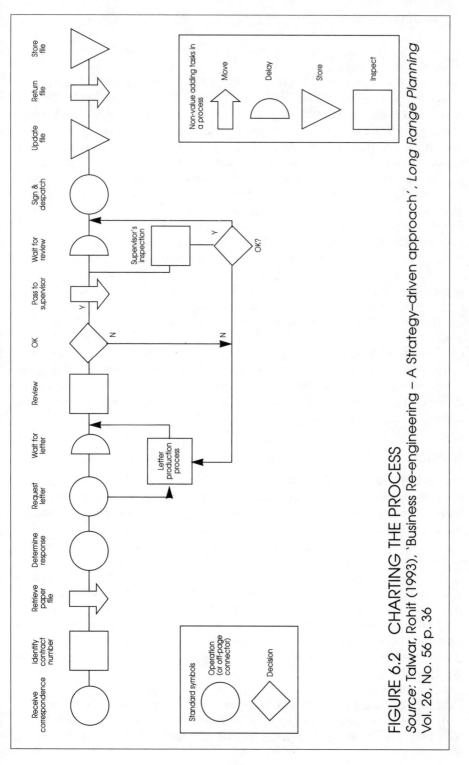

FIGURE 6.2   CHARTING THE PROCESS

Source: Talwar, Rohit (1993), 'Business Re-engineering – A Strategy-driven approach', *Long Range Planning*
Vol. 26, No. 56 p. 36

97

❖   **Health warning +**

Avoid paralysis by analysis as it is an expensive disease. But, remember, some analysis is very good for you.

Your analysis will throw light on the organization's deficiencies and suggest the scope for improvement and change. However, some organizations become paralysed by their in-depth study of existing practices. They run out of energy and resources to tackle the next stage of design and implementation. Remember, analysis gives you your starting point, not your destination. This is particularly the case when it is necessary to tear up existing processes and start from scratch. Beware of management consultants who make easy money from very bloated analysis. They produce piles of data that chart where you are going wrong in tremendous detail. They then explain the problems to you. They then produce recommendations that they leave you to implement. This is a phase fraught with difficulty where you might benefit from occasional outside advice and support.

The analysis will help you identify poor processes that may be better sourced out, rather than improved. If they are core to your business, you might have to think again about improving them or perhaps you need to re-examine what your core competencies really are. This analysis will probably point to more activities to divest in addition to those revealed from the review covered in Chapter 3.

Contracting out does not need to be restricted to low level activities. It can be extended to include leading edge functions such as design and engineering, as would be the case if you did not have adequate demand to merit employing the very best talent. Specialist design organizations can also work faster because of their experience and greater resources. Having the same resources in-house is unlikely to be cost effective.

REDESIGN

You should build a process redesign project team with staff from all the functions involved. It should include staff drawn from all levels. Some of the most useful ideas often come from junior members of staff. You should also seek to involve suppliers and ideally customers. The latter may not be practicable and in such cases it is vital to have excellent market research. You may well benefit from including outsiders who are not directly involved in processes. They are more likely to ask the obvious, fundamental questions that insiders take for granted. This sparks creativity that is most likely to stimulate radical solutions. Your project leader will need a good appreciation of re-engineering and to be supported by an expert who spreads knowledge to other team members. The team members should have good interpersonal skills and may need training in group problem solving. Chapter 4 on empowerment has much to offer on the working of such teams.

Re-engineering often means turning your back on past ways of working, by challenging assumptions. When someone explains that work is done in a particular way because it is accepted practice, ask the simple question why? Keep on asking that same question until you are satisfied with the answer. This will help you cut through the layers of tradition that may not add value to customers.

Customers dislike being served by several staff as this can result in needless delay, breakdown in communication and confusion. Where processes have become needlessly complicated this problem is typical. It happens when there is a single process for both very clear-cut cases and very difficult ones. Your objective should be to improve services to customers by reducing both the time it takes to complete the whole transaction and the number of staff they have to deal with.

You may gain from examining whether the work in a particular process falls into simple and difficult categories. If it does, you can design a simple process for the straightforward work and a more sophisticated approach for more demanding work. You can then try to restructure tasks so that the simple process can be handled by a case worker. This will reduce the need for coordination and speed up the process. If this is not possible, the next step in coping with complexity is to use a multi-skilled team. You may need to use functional experts for the most complicated processes.

You can save time by controlling work through reporting by exception. Traditionally much time is spent completing forms merely to show that work is going to schedule. You should aim to increase employee time spent with customers as processes are redesigned to minimize backroom jobs that are dominated by process and paperwork completed without much thought for customers. Design forms to map the process that are filled in only when there is a deviation. Important lessons can be learnt by analysing the reasons for variation.

Dramatic reductions in process time can be achieved by designing a process so that it can be carried out by one person, known as a case worker, rather than a number of staff from different departments. Such redesign will probably require extending the breadth of skills through multi-skilling. Skills can also be deepened by adding some former supervisor responsibilities for meeting output targets and quality. To this should be added the authority to make decisions and spend money up to agreed amounts without reference upwards. This allows the removal of double checking by more senior, better paid staff which usually costs much more than it saves. The number of managers can be reduced as there are both fewer distinct types of workers and fewer steps to coordinate.

If the process is beyond the capability of a multi-skilled case worker, a team approach is required. It may also not be cost effective to use a case worker if expensively acquired competencies are used very rarely. The same principle holds true for how far you go down the road of multi-skilling. Extended skills need to be used often enough for the staff to remain competent and confident. The time needed will vary from skill to skill as some staff will require more practice than others. The other factor to take into account is to ensure that the benefits of multi-skilling exceed the cost of training. There will come a point where it will be more cost effective for expensively acquired, infrequently used skills to be carried out by functional experts outside the team.

❖   **Health warning +**

There is a serious risk in designing-out all functional expertise.

While there are great benefits in replacing functions in a process by multi-skilled teams, make sure you also understand the extent to which functional expertise can be of value. There may be a case for keeping some functional specialists as consultants, who could have a research and development role linked with training and coaching.

Map the new process and compare the time taken, the number of steps and people involved with the previous process. Have you made the ambitious gains set out at the beginning? If not, start the redesign process again.

Information management and technology can be used to drive re-engineering and it will therefore be discussed during this phase. Examples of such projects are given in a later section of this chapter.

❖   **Health warning +**

Avoid expensive computer project failures by postponing this phase as long as practicable.

Many management consultancies and enthusiastic IM&T managers see re-engineering as an opportunity for massive new investment. In most cases you would benefit from piloting a new process and waiting until it has settled down as a fully operational system. This may result in further enhancements to the process. Starting the computing phase later could avoid a great deal of abortive work.

IMPLEMENTATION

It is crucial to test new processes thoroughly before they are introduced. The first step is to evaluate them in laboratory conditions. Once the process passes this test, it should be fully documented and the training programme developed. Select a pilot site where there are a few champions of the new; perhaps one member of the design team could be drawn from the pilot site. Staff will need to be trained and given enough time to come up to speed in the new process. They should be encouraged to suggest improvements to the new process.

It is important to look beyond the process itself, encompass empowerment and have regard to the need to design your reward strategy. This is tackled in Chapters 4 and 11.

INFORMATION MANAGEMENT AND TECHNOLOGY

The world of information management and technology is in a state of permanent revolution. Companies and technologies rise and fall with great rapidity. This section is a guide to some of your options and explains how you can side-step some very damaging pitfalls. It avoids a prescriptive approach as anything in print about IM&T is likely to soon date.

New IM&T is often a principal source of disappointment to the end-users. New programs may be out of date before they become live as they can take too long to write. Another problem is they may not be what users want. This can be because computer analysts often do not genuinely understand the process they are trying to support. Users also find it difficult to define their requirements in user specification and this results in further misunderstandings. Users and computer staff can sometimes end up blaming each other. They can be like an ill-suited couple on the dance floor inadvertently treading on each other's toes.

Rather than drifting into spending more on IM&T, you need to assess whether it can radically improve services to customers and/or reduce costs. One should recognize that in the past IM&T has failed to live up to expectations. According to Geoffrey Smart (1995) of Coopers & Lybrand in a review of the implementation of many hundreds of computer programs worldwide, some of the key problems have been as follows:

○ **Lack of clear project ownership**. It is essential to have a very senior member of staff who is fully committed to making the project a success.

○ **Lack of enthusiasm amongst users and changing targets**. This is often the case when systems are imposed on users without their involvement in the initial phases of the project, and particularly where there are clear 'losers' whose jobs or status will be adversely affected by the new system. Computer systems often concentrate on providing strategic and operational, gain at the expense of offering tangible benefits to staff lower down the hierarchy whose cooperation and commitment is essential.

○ **Large number of change requests**. This tends to happen if there is a lack of understanding of the work of the organization and its key processes.

Projects can also be developed on departmental and functional lines, merely replicating the clerical systems they replaced. Western Provident Association overcame this problem by making its programmers spend a third of their time doing users' jobs. Such a scheme greatly reduces the scope of misunderstanding and the many hours users spend agonizing about what they want the system to do for them. Wherever possible wait until a new process has been shown to work and is settling down well before computerizing it. You can then assess how the system can be improved further so that it does not merely computerize clerical processes. Look out for areas where computers can provide specialist information, and diagnostic and problem solving capability to staff which would contribute to their ability to combine a number of different rules. Another way to overcome these problems is to give users an early release of a part finished program. They can then quickly see what changes they would like made. This means that users have less time to wait for their new application.

How good is your IM&T department? Its capacity to meet your rapidly changing business needs may be compromised if it still has relatively inflexible mainframe systems. The danger is that by the time a new program has been written for you, your needs may have changed. How good is your IM&T manager? A few still have an introvert focus coupled with a desire to exert maximum control by imposing centralizing systems, even when there are other options. Jargon is used that acts as a barrier between them and their customers. Words like megabytes, C drives and file servers can be used to bring about a feel of inadequacy amongst users and increase their dependency on the expert. This allows the IM&T department to exert undue influence on the choice of systems, kit and software so that the user is left with what feels like work creation rather than a powerful tool in increasing their working effectiveness.

A different type of person is needed at the interface of the systems and the user. The skills required to be an effective programmer or analyst are often not compatible with those of highly-developed interpersonal skills, customer orientation and a participative approach to problem solving. Some organizations have bridged this gap by employing customer support staff who have an in-depth understanding of the systems and their applications, not only in their traditional role but promoting them into sales, marketing and systems development.

In spite of these weaknesses, there is good news as well. The increase in performance and the dramatic fall in the price of microcomputers is having a massive impact. They are cheap enough to have on everyone's desk. If the cost of Rolls-Royces had plummeted as far as computers, most drivers would buy a new car when it ran out of petrol! Microcomputers are powerful enough to do the work of many of the 'big boxes' of a few years ago. They can be reprogrammed quickly by customizing off-the-shelf programs. In-house programs can now be written much more quickly by using very powerful software tools. Staff may work on the same projects simultaneously through networks that can span continents. These trends are so dramatic that PC manufacturers have gained massive market share at the expense of producers of mainframes.

Computer networks and electronic mail can make the traditional middle management role of filtering and communicating information redundant. Increasingly, the middle tiers of organizations are being removed by delayering exercises, which will be covered in Chapter 10. You can communicate to all staff by sending e-mail messages. They could be regular updates on a serious development or perhaps, copies of press releases. E-mail gives you the scope to ensure that your staff never need to learn about what is going on in your organization in the press. Electronic mail can also be used as part of a staff empowerment programme (see Chapter 4). Computer communications can be invaluable to organizations that have many different locations. Staff in different parts of the country or overseas can contribute to a project by having immediate access to the same information database.

The success of electronic mail may depend on your organizational culture. It becomes very easy to copy people in to correspondence at the press of a button. This can lead to electronic 'back covering' to the extent that every morning you have fifty new messages to read through, of which only five are of value to you.

If your staff need to undertake some form of diagnosis or analysis, their work can be made much easier through using intelligent computer systems that flag the key questions and the probable answers. Your customers can get a quicker service as front-line staff do not have to refer difficult questions to supervisors or colleagues in different departments. Intelligent systems can empower front-line staff and result in further delayering of management. Insurance can be sold more cheaply over the phone than through agents who receive commission. Telephone sales staff use intelligent computer systems to offer tailor-made policies and process all aspects of the transaction.

Staff costs can be reduced by integrating computers and telephones. Job applicants can be routed through recorded questions that they will answer by pressing a number on the phone. If they get enough correct answers, they are sent an application form or in some cases booked into an interview. Curricula vitae can be electronically read and assessed, saving staff numbers. The program is sufficiently intelligent and flexible to pick up words and phrases that mirror the key ones that the recruiting organization is seeking.

IM&T can be the core of a re-engineering project as in the case of Merrill Lynch. The company improved its service to customers and reduced costs by eliminating clerical support through introducing an advanced computer system for retail brokerage. Errors were reduced by the software carrying out an elaborate series of checks. Brokers were able to use their work stations to enter orders for stocks. The system helped them to do their own clerical work for the first time. This saved 500 clerical jobs (*The Economist*, 22 February 1992, p. 82).

Your top management can improve their decision making through having access to regularly updated computer-based information. Communication can be improved by using graphics. However, your challenge is to turn the computer into a valuable, frequently used tool. It could very easily become the latest corporate toy that falls into disuse soon after it is taken out of its box. You may require a culture change as your top management might be very intuitive and make decisions without much hard information. One way to achieve this change is to target resources to support a few critical problem areas and demonstrate to them how this information can improve their decision making. You can use computers to improve control at all levels of the organization by supporting organizational strategies such as TQM. Such strategies often require the efficient capture and analysis of data on quality which is where computers come into their own.

You can reduce the size and cost of office space by staff, who do not have to be in the office every day, sharing desks. When they come into the office they can log into their computer database from whichever computer they use. This practice of 'hot desking' is most suited to staff who spend a large amount of time out of the office with clients or in the field, as say engineers.

They can also spend less time in the office by using computers at home or on the road. Staff can communicate with their colleagues through modems, faxes and mobile phones. Portable computers can be used by sales staff to produce quotations for their customers; sales details can then be passed back to the office for actioning. The sales persons' homes and cars are their offices. However, review thoroughly how you manage such staff by concentrating on agreed targets and deadlines. This approach gives staff the flexibility to work when they choose, providing they meet their objectives. Computers, faxes and mobile phones are being designed as one, lightweight device. Manufacturers hope that they will sell millions of them, which will further accelerate trends towards mobile working.

The need to travel to meetings can be reduced by video conferencing. This can be linked to an individual PC making dedicated studios less important. Medical services in remote areas are beginning to benefit from this type of technology. Video images of pregnant women are sent down telephone lines to the specialist Foetal Care Unit at Queen Charlotte's Hospital, London. This increases the speed of treatment and cuts costs. The implications are enormous as specialist centres potentially have a world market. This will increase their influence and income such that they can grow at the expense of some of their less prestigious counterparts. Could this trend effect your business?

The days of the dog-eared, out-of-date and expensive to update manual are coming to an end. Computer compact disks can store the contents of whole encyclopedias. Site engineers can have all the information they need at their finger tips. The training of staff at dispersed locations is made much easier through using interactive compact disks, which they can use on their own.

The Internet gives you access to tens of millions of people worldwide. It is no longer the preserve of computer nerds who prefer relating to computers than to people. Your organization can have its own shop window or site on the system for you to use for public relations purposes. There is a growing debate whether the Internet will take off as a medium for shopping. This depends on being able to 'send' money electronically with complete security. It has many possible other uses as a library at home as many publications have their back editions available on the system. It can also be used for recruitment. A London hospital faced with a serious UK-wide shortage of medical physicists recruited a candidate from Hong Kong using the Internet.

Organizations with millions of customers can sell to them as individuals. This can be done by using a computer to act as a data warehouse storing vast amounts of data and linking information from many different types of computers and programs that previously worked in isolation. Companies such as Tesco and British Airways are giving their customers incentives to join clubs that reward them for their purchases. Each time customers make purchases using a card encoded with their details, the organizational database is updated with their preferences. This information can then be used to target mailshots to customers who have brought similar products in the past.

Large amounts of information can be stored on smart cards. For instance, patients have been given their medical records on smart cards to carry with them. They do not have to wait for clerks to find their records when they go from the GP to hospital. Payments at places such as car parks can be made electronically without staff on site, with equipment that can handle cash, cheques and credit cards. This reduces the demand for clerical staff.

Computers also have a key role in computer-aided manufacture, computer-aided design (CAD) and flexible manufacturing, as we have already noted. The time required to design products can be greatly reduced by designers sharing a common database so that they can work in tandem using CAD. Computers can also be used to store off-the-shelf designs which can be tailored to meet specific customer requirements. Many more experimental designs can be produced as it is so much quicker than manual systems.

In spite of all the benefits computers can bring, beware of the 'toys-for-boys' syndrome. This happens when staff want the latest, fastest and best of everything, regardless of business needs. Computer equipment and software can become fashion objects. Those with last year's models can be looked down upon as if they were in a time warp – wearing 'flared' trousers! Then cost also includes lost time as some staff love using the new 'toy' in ways that are irrelevant to your organization such as changing the background colours of the computer screens.

It is essential to obtain independent, specialist advice on computers so that you do not buy a system that is already obsolete. The potential benefits and the number of applications of computer systems are growing rapidly as their costs fall dramatically and their performance improves.

MAKING THE LINKS WITH OTHER STRATEGIES

For re-engineering to succeed you need to ensure that the rest of your organization supports your new initiative. You will need to design jobs and structures that are sufficiently attractive to recruit and retain staff. You will also need thoroughly to review your training programmes to ensure that they provide your staff with the necessary new skills. This aspect is covered in Chapter 10. Your reward structure also requires revisiting to assess whether changes are needed there. This will be explored in Chapter 11.

Existing systems need to be mapped from prospecting for customers, through completing the transaction with the customer, to obtaining follow up business in the future. Critical tasks need to be highlighted, especially where the process tends to break down. The time taken to complete each step should be measured, along with the number of staff involved and the percentage failure rate for the task. Once this has been done you will know how long it takes to complete the entire cycle.

Flow charts are an excellent springboard to question why steps are taken and if they should exist at all, and whether work could flow differently. These and other valuable techniques will be covered in Chapter 8.

CHECKLIST FOR MANAGEMENT ACTION

1.   Energize
      ○ Ensure the active support of your chief executive.
      ○ Create a vision and translate this into clear objectives.
      ○ Set demanding goals.
      ○ Appoint a full-time project manager.
      ○ Appoint a process owner.
      ○ Establish your staffing flexibility, reviewing scope for early retirement.
      ○ Review your voluntary redundancy package.
      ○ Consider whether you need to freeze recruitment.
      ○ Design your communications strategy.

2.   Analyse
      ○ 'Walk through' your main processes.
      ○ Map them.
      ○ How long do existing processes take?
      ○ How many steps are involved?
      ○ How many times is work passed from person to person, i.e. how many hand-offs?
      ○ How much idle time is there when work has been handed-off to someone else's intray?
      ○ How many activities actually add value to the customer and what percentage of total time does this represent?
      ○ How many staff are involved in a process?
      ○ How much time can be saved by doing tasks simultaneously rather than sequentially?
      ○ Do you need to out source poor processes that would be difficult to improve?

3.   Redesign
      ○ Can you split tasks into simple, moderately difficult and complicated ones?
      ○ If yes, can you use case work for the easy ones?
      ○ Can a case worker deal with a moderately difficult task or do you need a multi-skilled team?
      ○ Can difficult cases be dealt with by a multi-skilled team or functional experts?
      ○ How can you ensure that you have some functional expertise to feed in new best practice?

4.   Implementation
      ○ Test your new process in laboratory conditions and adjust it as necessary.
      ○ Try it out on a pilot site – any further changes needed?
      ○ Train staff.

5.   IM&T

○ What is the scope for IM&T radically to improve your processes?

○ Can IM&T make caseworking possible?

○ Can you delay introducing IM&T until your new process has settled down?

○ Ensure that your programmers have actually seen and perhaps done the jobs they are programming.

○ Can computer programs be written quickly enough to meet your changing needs?

○ How can you enhance the productivity of your field and sales staff with IM&T?

○ What scope do you have for 'hot desking'?

○ Get independent advice to audit the effectiveness of your use of IM&T.

7

WHICH APPROACH TO CHANGE IS FOR YOU?

To know others is intelligence, while to know yourself
is wisdom

Chinese proverb

COMPARING APPROACHES

Gurus and their apostles preach empowerment, TQM and re-engineering
with religious fervour. They claim that their way is the only way. Any
deviation from their prescriptions by followers is a corporate sin for
which they will be punished in due course, encouraging a band of believers who
hang on every word of their gurus. Yet, in spite of paying homage to their idols
at international conferences, the organizational problems of followers refuse to
go away. So they reject that particular creed in favour of the latest offering.

We have presented a number of these approaches and their shortcomings in
previous chapters and you now have an understanding of what they can offer.
The different approaches are now coming closer together. TQM no longer needs
to suffer from being carried out within individual departments: it can be
extended to cover whole processes by using the re-engineering technique of
analysing processes with the use of flow charts. Empowerment can be given a
stronger customer focus by linking it to TQM.

Originally, re-engineering was presented as a top-down activity with values
and beliefs changing as an end result. The author of re-engineering has now
undergone a sea change in his thinking. James Champy in his most recent book
(1995) stresses the importance of cultural change and empowering the whole
workforce. He asks, how can managers who did so well under the old culture
show any enthusiasm for new approaches? How can the organization generate
trust after a blood bath of job cuts?

The answer is to invest in all staff, even those who are about to be made
redundant. This investment includes career guidance and extensive training
programmes that also equip staff for their future elsewhere, which might be with
another employer or as a member of the growing number of self-employed staff.
Thorn EMI provides an excellent case study of this type of approach, as was

illustrated in Chapter 2. You will receive much more support for change if you distribute some of the intended benefits to all your stakeholders. Find out what these benefits might be in advance through becoming closely involved with the agendas of customers, staff, shareholders, suppliers and the community. Are you prepared to rank them in this order? Many organizations believe that shareholders come first. They are then surprised when their customers desert them and their disgruntled staff wish they could walk out the door as well. Such a downward spiral is a problem that consultants are often called in to solve, yet the solution lies in the hands of organizations themselves. We recommend an upward spiral of delighted customers and motivated staff who then produce the returns for shareholders. You could also benefit from the long-term commitment of your suppliers. Winning over the local community will help in recruitment and should things go wrong at any point, it is likely to be much more sympathetic to your case, without need to resort to an expensive public relations campaign.

While giving equal prominence to the 'soft', human side of change by re-engineering is a welcome step, has it gone far enough? For instance, Champy states that followers are not to be commanded and controlled but understood. Organizations that convert followers into designers of change are at great advantage. They can channel the energy of staff who have a shrewd idea of what is wrong, what needs to change and how. To achieve this requires a significant investment in open, honest communication and extensive training as we saw in Chapter 4 on empowerment.

Criticism of re-engineered organizations is that they are superbly designed around current needs. They are often completely lean without any spare resources. Where will they find the people and the skills to transform themselves when the next challenge comes along? Have all their functional experts been replaced by multi-skilled staff with less knowledge and experience? Will there be sufficient flexibility to ensure that there will be enough staff to work in continuous improvement project groups? Procter and Gamble achieved large increases in productivity through empowerment yet chose not to slim down its workforce too far. Instead, it has the capacity to take people off the line and involve them in project and development work.

How do you take into account the impact of a rapidly changing environment when re-engineering a process? How do you plan for what you cannot predict? Implicitly, is not re-engineering best suited to stable, or at best, slowly changing environments? In turbulent times, there is a strong case to combine re-engineering and continuous quality improvement. That way, your organization can maintain its momentum for change after re-engineering has taken place.

Some re-engineering evangelists argue that TQM is dead. They claim that its incremental benefits are too small to gain an advantage in today's highly competitive market-place, that advantage can be achieved only by re-engineering. However, many organizations may not be capable of taking such a radical approach and the moderate benefits of TQM are better than nothing. The principles of TQM can be very useful to organizations that have re-engineered, by helping them to continue to improve their performance.

Now that you have reviewed empowerment, TQM and re-engineering in turn in the three previous chapters, you need to decide which approach or combination you wish to adopt. Empowerment probably has the lowest risk of failure. However you need to set this against the high degree of commitment resources management and staff time required, plus a large and ongoing investment in training. A degree of empowerment is essential for the delivery of re-engineering and TQM. While empowerment may bring only limited gains, it does reduce the risk of failing to implement change successfully.

In all the enthusiasm for change you can easily neglect to undertake a thorough evaluation. Without this you will be doomed to repeat the same mistakes again and again. Evaluation starts right at the beginning with carefully defined success criteria. These need to be translated into practical measures that can be reviewed on a before and after basis. You might consider involving an outside organization such as a business school that will offer a greater degree of objectivity.

There is a strong case for you to produce your own hybrid approach to change by relating the type of change you adopt to your own organizational needs. Table 7.1 shows you the impact of the different approaches to change to help you decide which one is most suited to your organization. Tick the description that most closely fits your situation and then 'cherry pick' aspects of each strategy to produce your own hybrid approach to change.

TABLE 7.1   DECIDING ON THE TOOLS OF CHANGE

Features	Business process re-engineering	✓	TQM	✓	Empower-ment	✓
What is the degree of commitment to change throughout your organization?	High		High to medium		High	
What is the direction of change?	Top down		Bottom up		Both	
Where is the ownership of change?	Top management		Everybody		Everybody	
What resources do you have available for implementation?	High, front end investment		Moderate, front end investment		High and continuous	
What is your commitment to training?	High		High		High	
What level of risk of failure to implement change can your organization sustain?	Very high		High		Medium to low	
How hierarchical do you want your organization to be?	Organized by processes not functions		Functionally organized with excellent communi-cations		Self-managed teams	
What level of staff participation are you seeking?	Moderate		Moderate to high		High	
What pattern of change can you live with?	Very discontinuous		Incremental		Incremental	
What level of potential benefits are you looking for?	Very big		Steady, small returns		Variable, but not short term	

CHECKLIST FOR MANAGEMENT ACTION

Table 7.2 provides an implementation framework that could support many hybrid approaches.

TABLE 7.2   PROJECT PLAN FOR IMPROVING PROCESSES

Phase	Activity
Set up project team	1. Establish project team
Assess the current situation	2. Determine customer expectations 3. Map the 'as is process' 4. Identify key success factors 5. Uncover possible root problems 6. Collect and organize product/process data
Designing satisfaction and speed	7. Redesign the product from the customer-for-customer perspective 8. Redesign the process for customer satisfaction and speed 9. Measure customer satisfaction, product quality, process and performance

Source: Robin Lawton (1992), 'Applying Customer-centred Quality to Human Resources', *National Productivity Review,* Summer

PART IV

UNDERPINNING CHANGE

Organizations exist to enable ordinary people to do
extraordinary things.
Ted Levitt, former editor, *Harvard Business Review*

8
TOOLS AND TECHNIQUES
FOR CHANGE

Follow the path of the unsafe, independent thinker.
Expose your ideas to the danger of controversy. Speak
your mind and fear less the label of 'crackpot' than
the stigma of conformity.
Thomas J. Watson, founder of IBM

Once you have chosen your approach to change, your next task is to
review the tools and techniques that can help you and your colleagues
to implement change successfully. In this chapter we will offer a very
wide range of tools and techniques so that you can select those that best support
your own strategy for change. Some of these tools are associated more with a
particular approach than another. But why miss out on an idea or a technique
that could benefit you? You may not use these tools and techniques yourself, but
you do need to know whether your staff are adequately equipped for this critical
phase of any implementation programme.

SELECTING TEAMS

❖   **Health warning +**

Beware cloning the strong aspects of your team; you may end up reproducing
the weaknesses too.

Creative and productive teams are likely to consist of a broad range of different
types of people. They will take time to settle down, going through phases of
forming, storming, norming and performing as members clarify their roles and
expectations. Try to avoid teams that clone a particular personality type as their
strengths are likely to be concentrated in a narrow area and they will have large
blind spots. It can be very pleasant to be a part of this type of team, but over
time this congeniality can accelerate the tendency of 'group think' with members
increasingly supporting each other's views even when they are out of step with
the outside world. It can be a nasty shock when reality hits.

When setting up a project team, you can improve its performance by having a wide range of personality types which all bring different strengths. Each personality type has a favoured role in the team. There are several different ways of categorizing team members. We have used the well-established typology developed by Belbin (Jay, 1995) which describes the different types as follows:

O   **Coordinator** – focuses on objectives, sets agendas and prioritizes objectives. Has personal authority and self-discipline. Gets the best out of people with a good feel for their strengths and weakness.

O   **Shaper** – quick-thinker and talker who provides structure to discussions and acts as a catalyst.

O   **Plant** – original thinker who provides new ideas.

O   **Monitor-evaluator** – analytical, counsels against risky solutions.

O   **Implementor** – practical, turns objectives into work programmes.

O   **Resource investigator** – explores new possibilities outside using extensive personal networks.

O   **Teamworker** – oils the team machine, helps team members to work well together.

O   **Finisher** – driven by deadlines and strong on following up tasks.

If your project team has difficulties in working, these may be a result of the composition of the team. If you think this is the case, consult Table 8.1, which suggests the most suitable personality types to improve specific aspects of team performance. Several organizations provide PC based tests that evaluate your team members and will help you in setting up and strengthening your team.

CREATIVE THINKING

Once you have built your team, you need to ensure that it is creative and can function quickly and effectively. Creative thinking is vital if you want to make a giant stride, rather than a series of small steps. It can be threatening as it often challenges the status quo. Creative thinking can be stifled if ideas that at first do not have the right feel to them are quickly ruled out. This problem occurs most often in groups made up of down-to-earth types that lack a member with vision,

TABLE 8.1   SELECTING THE MOST SUITABLE PERSONALITY TYPE TO IMPROVE TEAM PERFORMANCE

Problem	Personality types that can help most
Under-achievement	Coordinator; finisher
Conflict	Teamworker; coordinator
Indifferent performance	Resource investigator; plant; shaper
Mistake-ridden group	Evaluator; coordinator

the plant in the Belbin typology. Another problem is how to involve fully the lower status group members. Often, they have the potential to make the most valuable contribution because they are closest to the real problems, yet they may feel constrained by the fear of the consequences of contradicting their superiors.

A systematic approach to problem solving, such as the 'six hats' method of Edward De Bono avoids these problems (see Table 8.2). In the first instance, everyone in the group puts on a white hat and reviews what information is available and what new information should be collected. Moving to green hats means that emphasis is on new ideas and possibilities. Risk assessment and caution are considered when putting on black hats. The benefits are logically assessed with yellow hats. The whole process is considered during a blue hat phase. Some of the most creative ideas can come from intuition and emotions, without any need for justification, under red hats.

The advantage of the approach is that a much wider range of thinking is brought into play. It is also more constructive and problems can be solved more quickly as there is less scope for time wasting argument. It also lends clarity by simplifying the thinking process into a number of steps. Group members are likely to understand each other better as the more negative 'black hatted' types will have to try to see things from the point of view of the eternally optimistic 'yellow hats' and vice versa. For some this may be a new and difficult experience, all the more valuable because of it.

PROBLEM SOLVING

Where you will have workplace-based teams seeking to achieve continuous improvements, the following approach is recommended. It begins with team members identifying a major problem. They then write each of the different causes of the problem down on a Post-it. The facilitator or teamleader collects the Post-its and sorts them under headings. The team are then asked to use Post-its to list solutions. These are stuck next to the problem. Like the thinking hats, this process encourages each member of the team to participate, regardless of

TABLE 8.2   STIMULATING CREATIVITY THROUGH DE BONO'S THINKING HATS

Colour of hat	Type of thinking	Function
White	Neutral, objective	Obtain information
Red	Emotional	Show range and strength of feelings; provide drive, excitement
Black	Negative	Assess the case against and risk
Yellow	Positive, constructive	Provide vision, assess the case for
Green	Creative, lateral	Find fresh angles and alternatives
Blue	Directive, ordered	Structure and coordinate

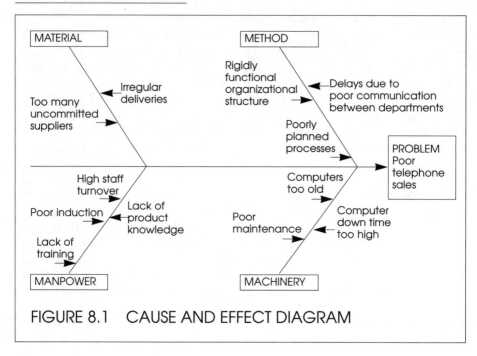

MATERIAL

METHOD

Too many
uncommitted
suppliers

Irregular
deliveries

Rigidly
functional
organizational
structure

Delays due to
poor communication
between departments

Poorly
planned
processes

PROBLEM
Poor
telephone
sales

High staff
turnover

Computers
too old

Poor induction

Lack of
product
knowledge

Poor
maintenance

Computer
down time
too high

Lack of
training

MANPOWER

MACHINERY

FIGURE 8.1   CAUSE AND EFFECT DIAGRAM

their status or the forcefulness or otherwise of their personality. It is called the cause and effect, or fishbone, diagram. It was originally extensively used in Japan and has since been used in TQM elsewhere (see Figure 8.1).

ANALYSING PROCESSES

FLOW CHARTS

Flow charts can show you where processes are unnecessarily complicated and involved. Where this is this case, they can be a powerful tool to demonstrate why change is needed. For the example shown in Figure 8.2 we have chosen a simple process of recruitment, as recruitment is something that we have all experienced at some time or another. It also does not involve a great number of steps. You will obtain greater benefits by selecting a process closer to your external customers and more mission critical to your organization along the lines suggested in previous chapters. However, if you work in personnel, this might be where you should start.

In our example, we have chosen to review and perhaps revise the person specification if we fail to attract the right candidate. It might be that we are seeking the impossible for the money on offer. It could be that the line manager is over-ambitious in the cluster of experience and skills he or she has specified. Some organizations just re-advertise in the hope of attracting better candidates. Looking at the example, we might ask, how often is authority not given to fill a

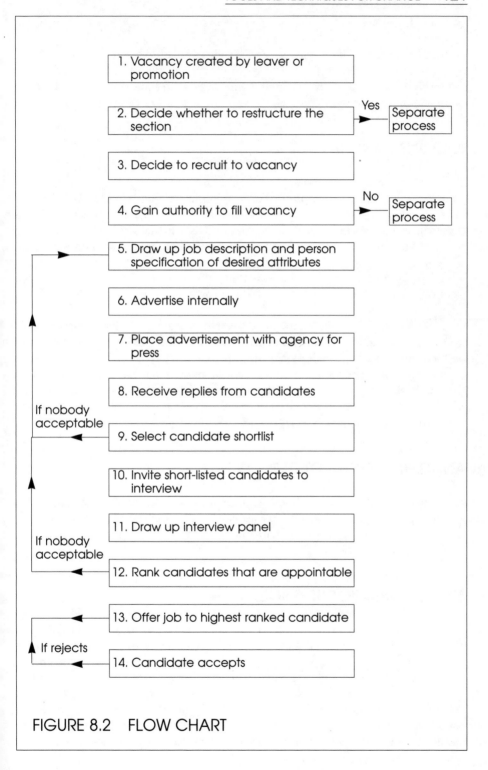

FIGURE 8.2   FLOW CHART

vacancy. If the answer is never, you might question why it is not cut out of the process, thus reducing the total time taken to fill a vacancy.

'Swimming lane' flow charts are designed to show where responsibility changes between departments. The more movement between them, the greater the scope for delay and error. Figure 8.3 illustrates the same example in the form of a swimming lane flow chart.

PROCESS ANALYSIS

Table 8.3 provides a process analysis of the recruitment example. It reveals that an activity that takes 30 elapsed days to complete requires under 21 hours (or three person days) of operational time and inspection. Thus productive time is slightly less than 10 per cent of elapsed time. This is actually quite high! For some processes the figure is 5 per cent. In our example the paperwork spends six days lying around in in-trays. Further delay is caused by the internal post. One option would be to include this in the equation by evaluating whether to introduce electronic mail. Contacting finance for approval, with associated delays, takes eight elapsed days.

A methodology for relating the activities in a process and relating them to time is shown in Table 8.3. This is particularly useful for identifying where there may be long time elapses, i.e. delays in the process.

For many processes you can add an additional column for 'Success rate'. This would be 100 per cent before the first step. You would then subtract the percentage of errors that occurred at each step. At the end of the process you will have the percentage of correct items as shown in Table 8.4.

ANALYSING PRODUCT DEFECTS

Concentration or 'chickenpox' diagrams are a useful and simple visual approach to fault identification. For each fault an 'x' is shown on the diagram so that the eye is immediately drawn to where the majority of faults have occurred. The sketch of a photocopier in Figure 8.4 illustrates its effectiveness.

SURVEYS AND FOCUS GROUPS

Surveys and focus groups are very important measurement tools to establish a before and after picture of the impact of a change initiative. Focus groups come into their own where issues are not clear-cut or are very sensitive. Focus groups usually consist of about eight people. They are led by someone who can subtly and gently encourage the less vocal members of the group to contribute and ensure that a few dominant personalities do not dictate proceedings. Therefore, psychology training can be very useful. The outcomes of focus groups are usually fascinating insights that can provide a useful guide to further action, but

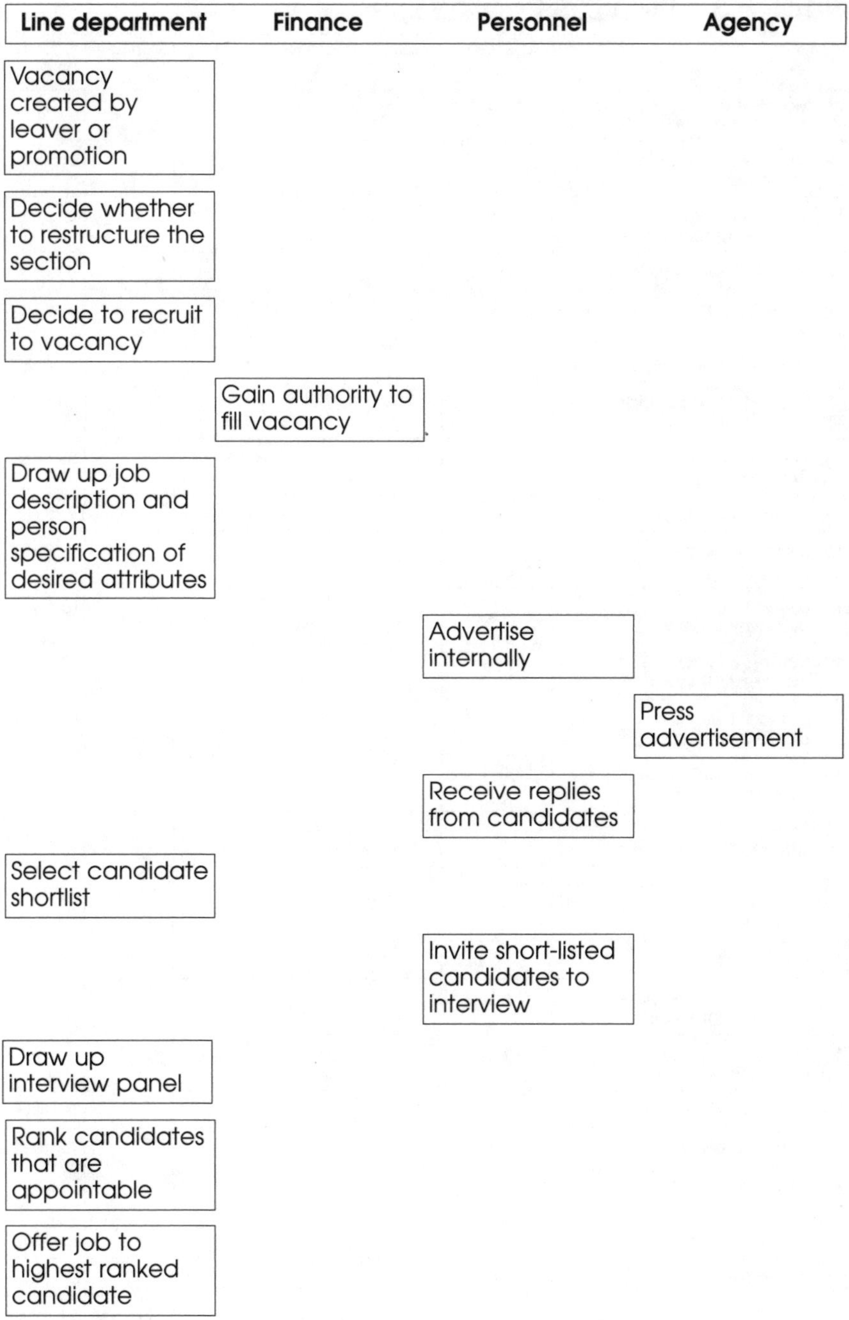

Line department	Finance	Personnel	Agency
Vacancy created by leaver or promotion			
Decide whether to restructure the section			
Decide to recruit to vacancy			
	Gain authority to fill vacancy		
Draw up job description and person specification of desired attributes			
		Advertise internally	
			Press advertisement
		Receive replies from candidates	
Select candidate shortlist			
		Invite short-listed candidates to interview	
Draw up interview panel			
Rank candidates that are appointable			
Offer job to highest ranked candidate			

FIGURE 8.3   'SWIMMING LANE' FLOW CHART

TABLE 8.3   PROCESS ANALYSIS

Activity	Operation	Inspect/ check	Transport	Delay	Storage	Elapsed time
1. Member of staff tells boss that they are resigning	5 mins					1 day
2. Manager rushes off to meetings etc.				2 days		3 days
3. Manager decides whether to restructure	30 mins					4 days
4. Manager writes to finance	20 mins					4 days
5. Letter sent in internal post			30 mins			5 days
6. Letter sits in in-tray				2 days		7 days
7. Finance check budget and decide		20 mins				7 days
8. Finance write to line manager	10 mins					8 days
9. Finance file reply	2 mins					8 days
10. Letter sent in post to manager			30 mins			9 days
11. Letter sits in manager's in-tray				2 days		10 days
12. Manager draws up job description etc.	60 mins					12 days
13. Manager sends details to personnel			30 mins			13 days
14. Personnel advertise internally	30 mins					13 days
15. Personnel fax advertisement to press			10 mins			13 days
16. Replies received and photocopied up to deadline	60 mins				10 mins	23 days
17. Shortlist selected	3 hours					23 days
18. Short-listed candidates invited to interview	2 hours					23 days
19. Phone candidates to invite them to interview	1 hour					
20. Candidates interviewed	9 hours					25 days
21. Rank candidates						25 days
22. Offer successful candidate job over phone	5 mins					26 days
23. Put offer in writing	20 mins					26 days
24. Post offer			1 day			27 days
25. Receive acceptance and photocopy to line manager	10 mins				10 mins	30 days
Total	20 hours 12 mins	20 mins	1 day, 1 hour, 40 mins.	6 days	20 mins	30 days

TABLE 8.4   PROCESS SUCCESS RATE

	Loss of quality at each step	Success rate
		100%
Step 1	–5%	
		95%
Step 2	–15%	
		80%
Step 3	–2%	
		78%
Step 4	–3%	
		75%
Step 5	–4%	
		71%
Step 6	–2%	
		69%

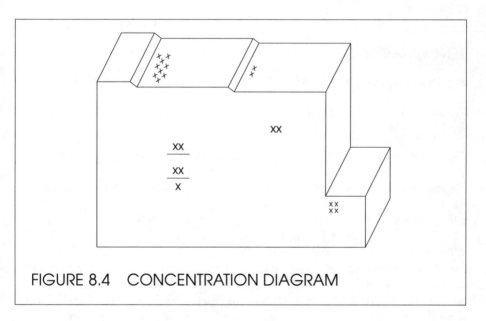

FIGURE 8.4   CONCENTRATION DIAGRAM

the number of participants is too small for their views to have statistical validity.

Surveys have the benefit of covering a very much larger number of people. They could be by personal interview or by postal questionnaire. Personal interviews are likely to have higher response rates as people find it harder to say no to someone than to throw questionnaires into the bin. However, personal interviews are more expensive. Whichever approach you use, make sure that the questionnaire is piloted so that confusing questions can be reworded. There is a real temptation to cutback or hurry this stage if deadlines are looming and to do so would almost certainly seriously compromise the results of the main survey.

Ensure that you use reputable independent organizations so that the results are more readily accepted by the sceptics.

❖   **Health warning +**

In-house surveys can appear to be a put up job and should therefore be avoided.

Surveys of customers are vital to give your organization a strong extrovert focus. You might think, why bother, if you receive regular reports from your sales force? While these are certainly useful, how objective are they? They may well centre on factors of immediate concern to the sales force so that you receive only a part of the picture.

Staff surveys allow you to explore issues of morale that are difficult to gauge otherwise. They can also indicate whether your strategy of, say, empowering your front line is working in practice. They can also test what staff think of your communications strategy. Such surveys can be used to help appraise the performance of managers through the eyes of their staff. We will cover this in Chapter 11.

BENCHMARKING

❖   **Health warning +**

Benchmarking others before you have benchmarked yourself gives industrial tourism a bad name.

Organizations use benchmarking to improve their performance by comparing themselves with 'best-in-class' practices. It can form part of a TQM, staff empowerment, re-engineering or a pick and mix strategy. Benchmarking can show you where your organization is strong or weak in terms of productivity, staffing levels and processes. The comparisons are usually made on a function by function basis, either within the same industry for key processes or between different industries for support functions such as personnel or finance. The attraction of benchmarking is that it can give your organization an extrovert focus so that it becomes less wedded to its own traditions. Benchmarking should be guided by your long-term strategy. In that way you can identify your organization's relative performance in those factors and processes critical for its success. Otherwise, it is easy to get drowned in detail that may be of little relevance to you.

Jonathan Weatherly defines three types of benchmarking as strategic, operational and organizational (Weatherly, 1992). Strategic benchmarking uses financial performance measures such as return on capital. Operational benchmarking compares the direct cost of a particular activity. Organizational benchmarking looks at the efficiency of the workforce and its indirect costs. For some measures, benefits might also be gained from making comparisons with different types of organizations.

Performance measures should focus on what has the biggest impact on staffing levels and production. One example is the number of employees for the personnel function. In manufacturing, measures would include productivity, defects, space utilization and time to produce an item. Involve staff themselves in devising measures best suited to their activities. The difficult task is to explain the differences between organizations. There may be several factors at work which can be difficult to separate, such as culture and training. Not all insights gained are suitable for implementing elsewhere. Even so, questioning existing practices and searching for new ideas will help keep an organization healthy.

A clearing house for collecting data in a consistent format and networking information to members has been set up in the USA. It has more than 100 members including IBM, Xerox and AT&T.

PITFALLS OF BENCHMARKING

Benchmarking does not encourage organizations to aim for market leadership, which requires being significantly better rather than merely matching best practice. It can easily degenerate into business tourism. It is at its most useful when you have a thorough understanding of your own organization. At this point, you will have a better idea of what are the critical issues that need to be investigated. Organizations with financial problems may be tempted to reduce staff to benchmark levels without further thought. Such action could undermine the effectiveness of the organization as the differences may be due to factors other than staff efficiency and effectiveness. An untypically large personnel department may not be overstaffed. It may be that it operates in a much tougher labour market and spends more time on staff retention issues and recruitment. A higher than average workforce in a factory may be caused by bad layout due to the constraints of old buildings rather than implying that something is wrong with the competence or motivation of staff.

If benchmarking is to be of real value, you must invest time and effort in understanding the real reasons behind organizational differences. Benchmarking is often used by TQM organizations, but some critics argue that it goes against the spirit of TQM, which should concentrate on ever-improving internal standards.

9

BECOMING MORE FOCUSED

The thinking was that we could do things jointly so
that the sum of two plus two made five instead of
four by exploiting synergies and economies of scale.
Jose Saavendra, Director of the Royal Bank of
Scotland Alliance at Banco Santander, on the mutual
benefits of this partnership

Having selected your approach to change, you need to make your organization more focused. You have re-assessed its strengths and weaknesses. Now you need to act on them. You might have to make difficult decisions about stopping certain activities and obtaining them from outside your organization. If you decide to set up alliances with other organizations you will be part of a growing trend. For instance, the number of US companies with formal alliances has increased from 750 during the 1970s to 20 000 in 1987–92 according to Booz, Allen & Hamilton management consultants (*The Economist*, 2 September 1995, p. 83).

THE NEED FOR ALLIANCES

Traditionally, the response to business success has been to expand by recruiting more staff and by developing support functions to service the key activities. In an attempt to control these larger structures, some organizations introduce more rules and regulations, which can make them into flabby, introverts, at the very time when they need a sharper focus to respond rapidly to the market changes that have threatened large, vertically integrated organizations. As a result, they fall behind nimble competitors.

Alternatively, growth can be achieved by taking over competitors and suppliers. Take-overs too can lead to failure or disappointment. The anticipated benefits may not be realized as the problems of mergers are often underestimated. There might be a clash of cultures between the organizations. Morale will usually decline in the organization that is taken over. Cooperation and output may sink to an all time low as staff fear for their jobs and mourn their lost promotion prospects. Another reason for failure is that purchasers may not have enough management resources to harness the new acquisition. Not surprisingly, many newly acquired organizations are often disposed of after a short period. Alliances mean that organizations can benefit from each other's strengths without the whole costs of a complete merger or take-over.

Staying small may not be the answer, on its own. The small may be at the mercy of the large and powerful. Another disadvantage of lack of size is that small organizations may well offer a more limited range of goods and services. In addition, they lack the financial, marketing and research capabilities of their larger competitors. How attractive it would be to have the benefits of size without its drawbacks. And here alliances and federal organizations prove their worth. Organizations can have most of the benefits of size yet remain slim through alliances, networks and the creative use of subcontractors. Alliances can vary in their duration, nature and extent. In the view of Harvard economist Robert Reich, except for high volume, capital intensive work 'every big company will be a confederation (or alliance) of small ones. All small organizations will be constantly in the process of linking up into big ones' (Reich and Mankin, 1986).

A powerful argument for forming alliances and subcontracting is to counteract the rising costs of research and development, tooling up production lines and launching new products. However, organizations have limited amounts of energy and resources, which are usually better used to build on success. It may be that there are no obvious quick ways to improve poor parts of the organization or its products. In this case then, these activities should be discontinued. Even successful non-core activities can be turned into autonomous units that also sell their skills to other organizations. Many organizations take this a step further, by developing only their core competencies and divesting everything else

The virtual organization is the most challenging example of the creative and extensive use of alliances. Organizations bring together a cast of professional and technical people to produce a particular product on a project basis. These are virtual organizations that last only as long as the project. The advantage of this approach is that scarce skills can be purchased only when they are needed. The organization remains dynamic as nobody is present long enough for powerful interest groups to emerge that become wedded to the status quo. Small management consultancies can act as virtual organizations. Sometimes they compete against each other while at other times they work together. This means that they can offer a wider range of expertise or more resources for large projects with tight deadlines. These consortia are headed by whoever wins the business, with the other consultants acting as subcontractors. These are fluid arrangements and the roles can be rapidly reversed.

Benetton, the clothing company, is an interesting example of an organization achieving greater corporate strength while contracting out to remain a small employer. Manufacturing is carried out under contract in many small factories and retailing is franchised, leaving the company with marketing, design and the running of controversial advertising campaigns. Communication is crucial to this type of organization. Manufacturers respond quickly to orders as they are generated by point of sale computers.

RELATIONSHIPS WITH SUPPLIERS

The typical Western view of subcontractors has been that they are eminently dispensable and can be chopped and changed for short-term price advantage. This approach often results in relatively short-term contracts that give suppliers little interest in investing time and effort in their customers. Suppliers as a consequence have little incentive to redesign their products and services to meet the needs of specific customers.

The Japanese, in contrast, see their suppliers as allies and establish long-term relationships based on a high degree of trust. Large companies such as Toyota are often supported by a web of suppliers. They provide mutual assistance and share commercially sensitive information. The stable and long-term relationships encourage improvements in quality. Also, costs can be reduced by suppliers designing components so that they are easier and quicker to assemble. Staff are sent on courses with each other's organization and work on joint project teams. Suppliers are more likely to locate themselves near their main customer if they have secured a long-term working relationship, thus reducing transport costs and facilitating teamworking between the two organizations.

Closer supplier relationships are essential for organizations implementing TQM, JIT and the demand flow approaches. They all place huge stress on making suppliers part of the team and signing them up to the same quality standards. The supplier should have systems to assure quality, which it should jointly seek to improve. If this is the case, the purchaser need not spend much time and effort monitoring goods or services received. Organizations may choose to contract out the monitoring of a supplier.

The main changes in the pattern of structures and alliances are summarized in Table 9.1.

TYPES OF ALLIANCES

There are many different types of alliances and some organizations engage in a wide range of different ones.

HANDOVER STRATEGIES

Goods or services are purchased from a supplier, usually in different businesses. The level of cooperation can vary. The strategy enables organizations to focus on their strengths. The ease of termination by the purchaser will depend on the depth of the relationship.

COMPLEMENTARY TRADING ALLIANCES

Complementary trading alliances can exchange technological advantage in one sphere for access to customers. Gaps in product ranges can also be rapidly filled by badging other manufacturers' products. There is often scope for economies

TABLE 9.1   CHANGING PATTERN OF STRUCTURES AND ALLIANCES

From	To
Vertical integration – doing most thing in-house	Specialization on core competencies – divest the rest
Strength through ownership	Strength through networks of allies
Suppliers are at arms length	Interdependence
Slowly evolving structures and relationships	Rapidly changing structures and relationship with some moving in the direction of the virtual organization

of scale as firms can withdraw from activities where their allies are better. This type of alliance requires patience while the allies improve the fit between their product ranges or styles of operation. There can be good opportunities to learn from each other. Such alliances are likely to become more popular as development costs increase and product life shortens.

Competitors with quite different strengths and weaknesses can form an alliance to provide complementary advantages. For instance, Apple had a very user-friendly microcomputer operating system yet had few big company accounts. IBM had a harder system to use. Apple was attracted by IBM's many large corporate customers and its mainframe computers that would fill a gap in Apple's product range. The two organizations have worked together on linking their computer systems, so there is a development aspect as well.

DEFENSIVE ALLIANCES

Competitor alliances can be established to counterbalance the influence of a dominant organization that poses a serious threat to its competitors. For instance, IBM wanted to lock out other manufacturers by introducing microcomputers with patented key components. The other manufacturers successfully ganged together to promote their own common standards.

RESEARCH AND DEVELOPMENT ALLIANCES

Economies of scale can be achieved where research is very costly or where there are marketing benefits in having products with common characteristics. Where the alliance is based around research, the relationship needs a long-term investment to develop the high degree of trust required. On the other hand, where the emphasis is on development, these arrangements can be loose ones, consisting of the sharing of patents, or selling licences to use them cheaply to competitors.

Philips formed a loose development alliance when it launched the compact disk player. As a result Philips was able to survive the Japanese competition that used its design format. This approach was learnt from bitter experience. When Philips prevented others from making compatible video systems, competitors devised their own. As a result, three incompatible systems found it difficult to establish themselves. After a very costly battle, the Japanese company with the most marketing muscle and lower production costs wiped out the Philips system, which was considered to be technically superior.

CREATIVE JOINT VENTURES

Creative joint ventures involve a substantial commitment by each party. Airbus is a good example of manufacturers grouping together to achieve economies of scale in an industry where the entry price for new entrants is massive. Only by joining forces could they compete with Boeing and McDonald Douglas, which are much larger than the constituent organizations of Airbus.

SERVICE ALLIANCES

Service alliances provide services to competitors that they find too costly to provide themselves, for example employers' associations might cover training. The Engineering Employers' Federation is a prominent example from the past. Its aim was to strengthen the position of smaller firms in their negotiations with trade unions.

LOBBYING ALLIANCES

Lobbying alliances are a specific type of service alliance dedicated to the role of pressure group. They often have the advantage of being able to claim that they speak on behalf of a whole industry. In addition they enjoy economies of scale and so are able to provide a higher level of service than members could afford on their own. For instance, the British Roads Federation encourages the government to spend more on roads and, conversely, Transport 2000 puts the case for increasing the investment in public transport.

BUILDING YOUR ALLIANCES

WHAT DO YOU WANT TO GAIN FROM ALLIANCES?

You need to have a well thought out strategy to identify what you wish to gain from your allies. The main benefits that can be gained from alliances, according to Dr Tom Sommerlatte and Edwin R. Stafford (Sommerlatte; Stafford, 1994) are as follows:

1.   Access to new markets.
     O   Reputation and brand quality.

    ○ Market access and knowledge.
    ○ Sales and service expertise.
2.   Acquiring technologies and skills.
    ○ Strategically critical manufacturing capabilities.
    ○ Research and development capability.
3.   Achieving economies and immediate financial support.
    ○ Low cost production.
    ○ Cash.
4.   Managing risk.
    ○ Common political needs and vulnerabilities.
5.   Reducing competition.
    ○ Similarly threatened by a more powerful competitor.

Which of the above benefits does your organization seek from alliances? Table 9.2 will help you select the types of alliances that might support your strategy. In some cases you can achieve the same outcome with different types of alliance, which gives you greater flexibility. Complete Table 9.3 for your own organization.

PARTNER SELECTION

Do not ignore 'soft' factors, such as different corporate cultures, in the excitement of seeking access to new markets or technology. If you ignore these issues you may fail to gain the hoped for benefits of the alliance. This does not mean that

TABLE 9.2   SELECTING THE TYPES OF ALLIANCES TO MEET ORGANIZATIONAL NEEDS

Type of alliance	Access to new markets	Acquiring technologies and skills	Achieving economies	Managing risk	Reducing competition
Handover strategy			x		
Complementary trading alliances	x		x		x
Defensive alliances				x	x
R&D alliances		x	x	x	
Creative joint ventures		x	x		x
Service alliances			x		
Lobbying alliances			x	x	

TABLE 9.3   SELECTING THE TYPES OF ALLIANCE FOR YOUR OWN ORGANIZATION

Type of alliance	Access to new markets	Acquiring technologies and skills	Achieving economies	Managing risk	Reducing competition
Handover strategy					
Complementary trading alliances					
Defensive alliances					
R&D alliances					
Creative joint ventures					
Service alliances					
Lobbying alliances					

you cannot work together with organizations with different cultures, but you both need to understand and respect each other's distinctive ways of doing things. An odd couple that have maintained their relationship are the youthful, maverick Apple computers and the more staid, blue-suited IBM.

What are the motives of your potential partners? It could be that they are seeking to obtain a short-term advantage at your expense. Both sides must be willing to work to achieve mutual trust. What do you need to do to win their trust and what should they do in return? Small steps will suffice in the first instance.

Work with your allies so that you share your visions and can develop compatible strategies. Alliances are unlikely to survive if one partner is moving up market at the very time the other is seeking to go in the opposite direction. Your staff also need to cooperate. You can foster cooperation with a joint communication and training strategy and by training staff together.

Take care to select relationships that are not balanced against you. Avoid much larger organizations or ones that would benefit much less than you from an alliance. They would have considerable power over you. They could walk away from the alliance without noticing much impact while their defection could be very much more serious for your organization.

NEGOTIATIONS

You should both make explicit what you hope to gain from an alliance and how you will assess and monitor this. You could ask each other, if this alliance works really well, what would we each gain and how would we ensure an element of fairness? Realism suggests that the divorce process is also clearly defined. You could clarify this with the question, if we were to have an amiable divorce, what steps would we each have to take to achieve it?

RUNNING THE ALLIANCE

To achieve the intended benefits of an alliance you need to turn strategic objectives into performance targets that you can carefully monitor. You could do this by setting up joint working groups with very specific objectives. Such groups will also help to improve understanding and trust between the two organizations. You also need to allocate resources, budgets and staff to make the alliance a success.

One of the main benefits of an alliance is corporate learning. Corporate learning can be maximised by having a significant number of staff working closely with allies. This avoids the risk of the loss of corporate memory that occurs when the few staff who have learnt crucial lessons leave your organization.

❖   **Health warning +**

Slow learners are the losers in alliances.

You need regularly to compare your strengths and weakness with those of your allies so that you do not lose out. You might suffer if your organization is slow to learn. You face the risk of being 'hollowed' out by your allies emulating your strengths before you have done the same yourself. Alliances can give access to core competencies, technologies and strategy. Japanese organizations learn very quickly and have outstripped many of their US allies. Complementary trading alliances can lead to one party becoming so dominant that it takes over production of the entire range of goods. The other ally is left as a sales agent, badging the other's products.

You can apply the lessons learnt in one product group very widely. Quite different products may benefit from the application of similar materials or production processes, allowing you access to a new and quite distinct market. The production of cars has been improved by adapting some of the technological materials used in the aircraft industry.

If you are a manufacturer that buys in large numbers of components from low cost suppliers through handover strategies, be alert to spawning new competitors. Your suppliers may extend their competencies to design and marketing so that they can make the complete finished product and sell it directly to the final customer. South Korean electronic companies have used this route to penetrate Western markets.

If your alliance lasts only a few years do not think it has necessarily failed. It

TABLE 9.4   ALLIANCE OBJECTIVES

Phase of alliance		
Mating objectives	Living together objectives	Mature relationship objectives
Month 1 month ?	Month ? month ?	Month ? month ?
1.	1.	1.
2.	2.	2.
3.	3.	3.

may be that it helped your organization to overcome a specific weakness much more rapidly than it could have done on its own. In this case, your alliance would have met its purpose.

Studies of why alliances fail show that too much is expected of them too soon. There is an overemphasis on short-term objectives and profitability. Cooperation between allies may suffer from a clash of cultures that takes time to resolve. Therefore, set easy objectives in the first, mating phase. More demanding objectives can be mapped out for the living together stage. Reserve the most demanding ones for when you have established a mature relationship. You also need to decide together how long each phase is likely to last. Completing Table 9.4 will help you set your alliance objectives.

CHECKLIST FOR MANAGEMENT ACTION

1.   Decide on strategic requirements for alliances.
     Once you have a clear idea of what you want to divest and where you
     are weak, you will have a clearer idea of what type of alliance(s) you
     want. The SWOT and PEST analyses that you completed in Chapter 3
     will have provided you with a good idea of your requirements.
2.   Decide on the types of alliances.
3.   Select a partner.
     The compatibility of cultures and shared vision between you and a
     potential ally will have been influenced by your choices on
     empowerment, TQM and re-engineering (Chapters 4, 5 and 6).
       Look out for an organization with:
     O Compatible cultures;
     O Shared vision;
     O Compatible strategic goals.
4.   Negotiate alliance.
5.   Be very clear what you want out of the alliance and turn this into success
     criteria that can be monitored
6.   Running the alliance
     O Commit adequate staff to work closely with allies.
     O Learning from your allies should be high priority.
     O Guard against the loss of corporate memory by trying to retain
        liaison staff.
     O Monitor performance of the alliance against success criteria.

10

DESIGNING JOBS AND STRUCTURES

> We trained hard, but it seemed that every time we were
> beginning to form into teams, we would be reorganised.
> I was to learn later in life that we tend to meet any new
> situation by reorganising, and a wasteful method it can
> be for creating the illusion of progress while producing
> confusion, inefficiency and demoralisation.
> Gaius Petronius, AD 60

Whichever approach you select to managing change within your organization it is vital that the structure you choose facilitates rather than inhibits the change. Roles and jobs must be designed so that the essential attributes of successful organizations such as customer focus, flexibility and openness to the environment are clearly supported. Whilst structures will change and evolve over time they should not be reorganized with regular monotony. The words of poor old Gaius Petronius are as true now as they were in AD 60; constantly restructuring is no substitute for achieving meaningful second order change.

This chapter summarizes the evolution of organizations as we know them today and puts forward alternative structures that will facilitate organization change. It also highlights different ways of arranging roles and jobs.

THE EVOLUTION OF ORGANIZATIONAL STRUCTURES

As organizations grow beyond the capacity of the original founder to manage all the staff directly, departments are set up. They are usually based on function, such as production, sales and accounts. As the organization grows larger still, the departments are subdivided into sections. In that way it is possible to be able to afford to employ specialist skills. The organization becomes more introverted as more and more staff work in head office functions, relatively isolated from customers and the production of goods or the supplying of services. This is the basis of the self-defeating, introvert focus mentioned in Chapter 1.

Another feature of the hierarchy is the difficulty of coordinating the various functions, especially when new products are devised and introduced. The many departments involved have their own priorities and agendas that may pull in different directions. Some organizations tackle this problem by having product divisions. For instance a computer manufacturer might have separate divisions for mainframe, mini-computers and microcomputers, each with their own sales force, finance and personnel functions. This structure has the advantage that new products can be developed faster as there are shorter lines of communication. Against this, it is costlier to have support services in each division than in a centralized department. Also, isolated professionals may stagnate without the stimulation from colleagues that working together at the centre provides.

Matrix organizations seek to get the best of both worlds by combining function with product or project management. Thus a senior engineering manager may also head up a multidisciplinary team in charge of a new project. This type of organization overcomes many of the disadvantages of functional and product basis structures, although there may be conflict between the two managerial roles. A matrix organization can be costly as it may require more senior staff.

What is apparent is that a new type of organizational structure is needed to meet today's changing environment, and the evolutionary process must continue.

MEETING TODAY'S CHALLENGES

The clear message coming from most management gurus is that the hierarchical organization will wither away because it is unable to respond to the risk factors highlighted in Chapter 1. Hierarchical organizations cannot satisfy the more quality conscious customers because of their functionally fragmented processes that lead to demarcation disputes, the 'it's not my job' mentality. Their convoluted management processes cannot meet demand from more sophisticated customers for an ever-expanding product range. The shortened life cycle of products and services and technological obsolescence cannot be easily accommodated by organizations that are geared to maintaining the steady state. The more introverted centralized organization is slow to respond and may not even see new more flexible entrants to the market.

The new dynamic, flexible, staff-involving customer-oriented, highly productive organization will be different – but what will it look like? We do not know yet but some points are beginning to emerge.

Rosabeth Moss Kanter argues in her book *When Giants Learn to Dance* (1992) that winning the new game requires faster action, more creative manoeuvring, more flexibility, and closer partnerships with employees and customers than was typical in the traditional corporate bureaucracy. It requires more agile, limbo management that pursues opportunity without being bogged down by cumbersome structures or weighty procedures that impede action.

Thomas A. Stewart (1992) identifies three main changes.

1. The 'high involvement workplace' – organizations with self-managing teams and other devices for empowering employees.
2. A new emphasis on managing business processes, e.g. materials handling rather than functional departments like purchasing and manufacturing.
3. The evolution of information technology to the point where knowledge, accountability and results can be distributed rapidly anywhere in the organization.

HORIZONTAL ORGANIZATION

Frank Osstreff and Doug Smith, consultants with McKinsey and Co., have prepared a 10-point blueprint for the horizontal company which they see as 'perhaps the first real fundamentally different robust alternative' to the functional hierarchical organization.

McKinsey and Co.'s 10-point blueprint for a horizontal company (Osstreff and Smith 1993)

1. Organize primarily around process, not task – base performance objectives on customer needs. Identify the process that meets these needs and then these processes become the company's main components.
2. Flatten the hierarchy and reduce the size and scope of functional departments. Create teams of multi-skilled staff to cover whole processes that were previously split between different departments and teams.
3. Give senior leaders charge of processes and process performance.
4. Link performance objectives and evaluation of all activities to customer satisfaction.
5. Make teams, not individuals, the focus of organization performance and design.
6. Combine managerial and non-managerial activities as often as possible, i.e. let workers' teams take on hiring, evaluating and scheduling.
7. Emphasize that each employee should develop several competencies. You need only a few specialists.
8. Inform and train people on a just-in-time, need-to-perform basis.
9. Maximize supplier and customer contact with everyone in the organization.
10. Reward individual skill development and team performance instead of individual performance alone.

THE LEARNING ORGANIZATION

Mike Pedler, John Burgoyne and Tom Boydell in their book *The Learning Company* (1991) describe the learning organization. It is based more on a philosophy than any particular organizational design. They state that learning organizations are those that are capable of adapting, changing, developing and transforming themselves in response to the needs, wishes and aspirations of people inside and outside. They will be able to avoid the sudden and massive restructuring that happens after years of not noticing the signals.

Pedler *et al.* define the characteristics of the learning company as follows:

1.   The company policy and strategy are formulated together. Implementation, evaluation and improvement are consciously structured as a learning process.
2.   All members of the company have a chance to take part, to discuss and contribute to major policy decisions.
3.   IM&T is used to inform and empower people.
4.   All internal units and departments see themselves as customers and suppliers, contracting with one another. This forces all groups to engage in constant dialogue.
5.   The reward strategy should be flexible so that it actually reinforces the agreed priorities of the organization.
6.   Structures should be designed to create opportunities for individual and business development.
7.   Scanning the environment is carried out by all members who have contact with external customers and is used to inform the business strategy.
8.   The organization will engage in joint learning opportunities with its competitors and allies as it seeks to delight its customers.
9.   Managers will create a learning climate by making their primary task the facilitating of staff members' experimentation and learning from experience.
10.   Resources and facilities for self-development are made available to all members of the company.

SHAMROCK STRUCTURE

Charles Handy considers that it is possible to combine the advantages of being small and autonomous with the economies of scale of large organizations through federal structures. In *Age of Unreason* (1991) he describes the concept of a shamrock organization. A shamrock organization has three distinct components: core professional employees; the contractual fringe; and the flexible workforce.

Core workers, the first leaf of the organization, are the star players on whom the organization depends for its success. They are usually highly qualified professional and technical staff. Their potential value to competitors means that their employers seek to retain them by giving them special treatment, as reflected in their reward packages. In return, they are very committed and work long hours. Due to the cost of core workers, they represent a shrinking minority.

The second leaf of the clover is contracted-out services. Obvious examples of this are catering and security, yet, increasingly, more aspects of large organizations such as payroll services are being contracted out. Some organizations have gone to the extent of contracting out much more sophisticated services such as engineering design and IM&T. The service levels and results that they are expected to achieve are written into the contract with the supplier. The suppliers are paid on a fee basis and failure to meet agreed standards may result in reduced payment and the loss of the contract.

Some organizations encourage their staff to form their own companies and bid for contracts with their former employer; they may even be guaranteed a certain volume of business for a transitional period. Other organizations such as local authorities and the NHS put the work out to contract, which could be won by an in-house bid or an external contractor.

Part-time and temporary workers make up the third leaf of the shamrock organization. They can be an important means of meeting seasonal, weekly or daily peaks in demand, particularly in retailing and the service sector. There is also a growing demand from delayered organizations for interim managers as they have no spare resources for special projects and developments. This type of employment is popular with women returning to work after career breaks. It also gives both men and women scope to support themselves when less dependable and predictable careers in fields such as the arts fail to do so.

Handy talks about a fourth leaf of the clover. This is where customers do work themselves that previously was done for them. Thus, motorists have become their own petrol pump attendants, and family and friends nurse patients who are discharged from hospital much earlier than in the past.

The real question is how to combine all of these theories into a practical, understandable design that will be the blueprint for organizations in the twenty-first century. How do we relate these main thrusts to the approaches pursued in Chapters 4, 5 and 6 and design the jobs and structures to turn them into reality? Let us explore this question in relation to empowerment, re-engineering, TQM and pick and mix.

EMPOWERMENT

In Chapter 4 we listed the vital ingredients for empowerment as follows:

O   Employee involvement.
O   Management support.
O   Employee information.
O   Appropriate training.
O   Compatible organizational systems.

Any structure chosen to facilitate the empowerment approach must be able to incorporate most of these factors and should support the free flow of information both up and down and laterally. Then all staff will have sufficient information available to them to feel involved and able to contribute towards decision making. The maximum devolution of authority and accountability to the staff actually doing the job will also be required. The role of managers will need to change from command and control to facilitating, coaching and resourcing. Positions in the hierarchy need to be governed more by what you know than by time served and perceived status. Self-managed teams are felt to achieve the best climate for total empowerment but may be too counter-cultural for all organizations to move to in one step. Chapter 4 suggests different levels of empowerment depending on the underlying culture in your organization and you should review this point when considering your new structure.

TQM

Total quality management is often overlaid on existing jobs and structures, but jobs and structures can be redesigned to facilitate the main aims of TQM. These aims were identified in Chapter 5 as follows:

O   Customers must come first.
O   A quality culture must be led from the top.
O   Good communications between divisions and departments.
O   Beliefs and values which support the quality culture.
O   Each member of staff is responsible for the quality of his or her own work.

We can see from this list that a participative management style and fewer layers of managers are essential ingredients. To produce quality services and products staff must by definition be competent. Reward strategy, of which paying for knowledge is one example, needs to be consistent.

RE-ENGINEERING

The term re-engineering encapsulates one of the main thrusts highlighted by Rosemary Stewart. It forces the organization to think about the primary processes: the tasks involved in supporting these processes; the translating of these tasks into roles and jobs; and then designing a structure that supports rather than hampers the processes.

It has been demonstrated that some early re-engineering attempts ignored or at best underestimated the importance of the human aspect. Leicester Royal Infirmary, an example of healthcare re-engineering, attributes 75 per cent of its success to social and cultural factors and only 25 per cent to rationality and analysis. A survey conducted in 1994 by M. Oram and R. Wellin for their book *Re-engineering's Missing Ingredient: The Human Factor* (1995) indicated that managing change is the toughest challenge for re-engineering. They advocate that not only processes should be examined but also the structure, the design of jobs, new approaches to selection and training and changed performance management, etc.

Wellin and Rick (1995) record that the Royal Bank of Scotland, when it conducted a fundamental review of its business, identified its key problems as follows:

O   Poor organizational design.
O   Poor quality people in key positions.
O   Lack of vision and investment in IT.

O   Unreliable lending and pricing policies.
O   Unimaginative products.
O   Low priority given to customer service.

It found that to achieve successful change required changes in every facet of bank life but in career management in particular. It had to introduce the concept of lifelong employability rather than lifelong employment. It had to develop role definitions that would lay the foundations for new career paths and different families of jobs. These were all based on a competency framework that described roles in far greater detail, looking not just at *what* has to be done but also *how*.

When you are re-engineering, new processes must be supported by changes in behaviour and roles. Meeting customer needs can be facilitated by increasing the amount of time staff spend with them. Support staff who have very little customer contact not surprisingly give a higher priority to their own paperwork than customers, who are often seen as a nuisance. These roles need to be designed out as much as possible.

Customer satisfaction is significantly increased by effective transactions performed without delay by as few people as possible. Multi-skilled staff with the competencies required to complete the transaction can achieve this aim. However, there are limits to multi-skilling based on the cost of the additional skills in relation to the frequency of use.

As well as multi-skilling, staff will require information both to handle the transaction and to deal with subsequent problems. The ideal way to supply the information is through information technology. High level diagnostic skills may be implemented through the use of computer-based artificial intelligence. For example, Direct Line insurance uses a computerized decision tree to enable one member of staff to supply an insurance quotation. A high, continuing investment in training is required.

Discretion is an important element when dealing with the majority of everyday problems. Customer-oriented organizations permit front-line staff discretion, for example an electricity company allows its staff to decide whether to give customers rebates when price queries have arisen. The level of discretion needs to be explicit and staff need the confidence to use their discretion appropriately.

Teamworking is used where it is not cost effective or sensible for one member of staff to possess all the competencies for a transaction.

The role of management becomes more to facilitate and less to coordinate and control. Jobs will evolve and are not frozen in job descriptions. They should be inherently satisfying without being dominated by short-cycle, repetitive tasks. Reward and appraisal systems will need to support teamworking and meeting customer needs. The emphasis will need to move from inputs to output and outcomes, which could be reflected in the reward structure.

PICK AND MIX

With the pick and mix option an organization is not restricted to particular job designs or structures but can select from the total menu.

Case study: Restructuring and reducing cycle time – ABB

The Swedish-Swiss engineering combine, ABB, is aiming to reduce all its lead times by 50 per cent. The reduction will be achieved by decentralizing specialist skills, multi-skilling, and high performance teams. The teams consist of 10 to 15 members and replace fragmented departments. They have greater responsibility for administration with layers of managers removed. Blue- and white-collar distinctions were removed with the harmonization of pay and conditions. Supervisors are to be turned into coaches and will rotate between teams. A base line of workshop attitudes was established by an independent survey. There remains only three layers of management for a $30 billion organization. It consists of 13 executive committee members, 250 senior managers (business area and country chiefs) and 5000 business managers. There are less than 150 staff at headquarters. Regional offices have five or six staff. A significant advantage of ABB is that it was already very decentralized. Trade unions have been fully involved in all changes.

ABB has a global matrix structure with operating companies reporting to a regional manager and a worldwide business head. ABB can therefore act globally and locally. Top managers are charged to ensure that the 1300 companies benefit from each other's core competencies. These companies are encouraged to act enterprenuerially. They can borrow money independently and retain a significant amount of their earnings.

Sources: Hans H. Hinterbuber and Boris M. Levin, (1994), *Long Range Planning*, Vol. 27, p. 46; and Anat Arkin (1995), 'Self-renewing Companies', *People Management*, 19 October, p. 37.

❖   **Health warning +**

There must be compatibility between job design, structures and organizational systems.

DELAYERING

Those organizations that do not want to restructure totally can still benefit from a flat structure with the minimum of tiers. The process of removing surplus levels of the organization is called delayering. Its benefits can be found in the following:

O   Less overlap between the different levels.
O   Faster decision making.
O   Lower management costs.
O   Greater individual discretion and accountability.

One approach to evaluating the number of tiers needed is to start at the bottom of the organizational hierarchy. Broaden out these jobs, if you feel that the existing staff can do them with more training. If it is necessary to recruit different types of workers, this will be dependent on cost and their availability in the labour market.

Once you have broadened out the bottom tier, consider what management functions it requires and how could they be best provided. The exercise can be repeated for the next tier.

The maximum span of control depends on the type and location of work undertaken. Peters (1993) considers that there ought to be one supervisor to 25 to 75 non-supervisors. He argues that this huge span of control facilitates devolving responsibility to non-supervisors.

The downside of downsizing

While an organization may benefit from being scaled down, there is a risk that this can be taken too far. The purpose of restructuring is to improve quality and reduce costs yet a US study of 1000 companies showed that only 191 reported that they were more competitive after downsizing (Tomasko, 1992).

A scaled-down organization needs to work in new ways, otherwise the remaining staff struggle unsuccessfully with the increased workload. There are no longer the resources to meet fresh challenges. One response to more failure is to slim down further until the organization virtually disappears – excessive downsizing leading to organizational anorexia. Another response, should the organization survive, is to replace the redundant posts. The fundamental reason

Case study: British Telecom – Project Sovereign

The objective of Project Sovereign was to make BT more customer-driven and reduce costs. The project was owned and driven by the chairman, who ran the control board, which was managed on project lines.

The detailed changes were devised by 15 project teams managed in different parts of the country. Hundreds of staff were involved at all levels; some on a part-time basis and others full-time. Activity analysis was undertaken of current activities along with zero-based planning.

Products were brought together in a portfolio as a coherent range, rather than being managed as separate entities. Consumer-facing divisions were set up, i.e. personal communications, business communication and special business such as Yellow Pages and operator services. The management of national and international networks was unified.

Structures were flattened out to a maximum of six levels instead of ten or eleven. 38 000 managers were re-appointed over a ten-month period. All were put through a training programme. 6000 managerial jobs were lost. An attractive severance package was on offer and there were no compulsory redundancies. Thus trade unions were reasonably supportive.

Surveys were undertaken of staff attitudes before, during and after the changes in order to monitor their response.

Source: British Telecom

for such failure is that organizations continue to work in old ways, but with fewer staff who become overworked and exhausted.

Other problems include the loss of organizational memory due to the departure of too many experienced staff. Staff morale may plummet if staff reductions are handled badly. The surviving staff may feel very insecure and put their energies into finding new jobs. Their prime concern at work is to stop taking risks so that they avoid the possibility of being blamed for failure.

Most failed downsizing exercises are obsessed with reducing headcount. Instead, organizations should concentrate on becoming more responsive to customers, eliminate unnecessary processes, multi-skill staff, then delayer, along the lines set out in this chapter.

CHECKLIST FOR MANAGEMENT ACTION

The following guidelines will help you redesign jobs to enhance organization flexibility and speed of response.

1. Enhance customer focus by increasing the percentage of time spent with customers by computerizing or designing out much administration.
2. Solve problems quickly by empowering staff with higher levels of discretion with information at their finger tips:
    ○ IM&T systems and skills;
    ○ much smaller role for supervision.
3. Reduce delays through fewer hand-offs by:
    ○ multi-skilling;
    ○ teamworking.
4. Increase flexibility by creating organic jobs to replace the rigidly defined job description mentality.
5. Support staff by:
    ○ more and better training especially on-the-job training;
    ○ managers become more like coaches.
6. Improve quality by making jobs more interesting by adding variety and avoiding short-cycle, repetitive tasks
7. Manage performance by moving from monitoring inputs to output and outcome orientation.

11

REWARD STRATEGY

Staff are your only assets that stage a mass walk out
every night. Some, however, don't come back.

Many organizations have treated reward strategy as a panacea, in the belief that it can cure all their ills such as under-performance. It is often assumed that it is a matter of picking the winners and losers in an organization and rewarding and punishing them accordingly. Some feel that reward is a gilded carrot that entices the rabbits to improve their performance. Non-performing rabbits are to be caught in the searing headlights of an individual performance review. If they do not respond, the least fluffy of them are run over. The biggest mistake some organizations have made with reward strategies is to assume that they are an end in themselves. Rather, they are a means of supporting the organization's long-term objectives. This is why we are introducing the subject at the end of our guide to organizational change. We will take you through the numerous reward options and help you select those that are most in tune with your change strategy.

If you have changed your organizational structure you need to review its impact on reward strategy. For instance, if you have delayered your organization some of the rungs up the promotional ladder will have been sawn off. Staff will be demotivated unless you give them better rewards for doing well in their current jobs. You can supplement rewards with a greater investment in training, staff development and lateral moves. Restructuring or changes in market forces can increase the value of certain jobs, making you more vulnerable to staff turnover. Merrill Lynch faced this problem with its stockbrokers. It introduced a company bonus of $100,000 for those who stayed with the company for ten years and met certain performance criteria (Milkovich and Milkovich, 1992, p. 54).

❖ **Health warning +**

Some strategies risk failure as they are introduced too quickly and without adequate thought, often to signal a break with the past by a new chief executive.

Reward strategy covers pay as well as the wide range of possible fringe benefits. We will concentrate mainly on the pay aspects or this chapter could become a book in its own right. There are many types of reward strategies. Staff can be paid for the job, for possessing skills and according to their performance, or even a combination of these.

Reward strategy is often used as a vehicle for bringing about change as it tends to spotlight the top management agenda. It has been used to try to improve both productivity and the motivation of staff. It highlights the chief concerns of organizations and 'what gets measured gets done'. (Redmand and Snape, 1992). The corollary of this is also often true: what doesn't get measured doesn't get done! Some of these ignored activities could be very costly to your organization. Sales staff paid according to their sales figures can actually drive away customers. Many potential customers are deterred from entering a car dealer's showroom. They wonder, are they going to be attacked by an alligator or enmeshed in a tarantula's web? One manufacturer, Daewoo, turns this to its advantage by advertising to the public that its staff receive no commission and are there only to answer your questions.

There has been much interest in linking performance management to reward strategies with performance-related pay. Now there is considerable controversy about its value. There is also much debate about the merits of different forms of staff performance management systems and reward strategies. Clearly there is no ideal approach that fits all organizations. Some organizations even have different strategies for each type of staff. You need to select a way forward that best suits your organization's requirements and carefully monitor the results. You will certainly benefit from the active participation of your personnel director in shaping your reward strategy. He or she should be able to provide you with a detailed analysis of the costs and benefits of your existing packages. Reward is too important to be left to personnel staff, however, particularly at a time of major change.

OBJECTIVES OF REWARD STRATEGY

Use your reward strategy to reinforce your organizational goals. Examine them closely to ensure consistency. In some organizations the overall strategy and reward strategy are actually in direct conflict. For instance some organizations have introduced individual performance pay while seeking to encourage teamworking!

There are many possible objectives of a reward strategy. Use Table 11.1 to rank yours, marking 1 against your first choice. Start with your current strategy and then repeat the ranking for your future strategy.

How consistent are your answers? Are they overambitious? Are you expecting too much from your reward strategy? Are there large changes between your current and future strategies? Now write down your objectives, using Table 11.2, and against each put the measure you will use to assess its effectiveness. You should then decide what the pass mark should be. An example would be to

TABLE 11.1   OBJECTIVES OF YOUR REWARD STRATEGY

Objective	Ranking	
	Current	Future
Improve productivity		
Improve quality		
Improve retention of key staff		
Support multi-skilling		
Enhance teamwork		
Improve individual performance		
Increase staff commitment to the organization		
Change organizational culture		

TABLE 11.2   ESTABLISHING SUCCESS CRITERIA

Objective	Measure	Pass mark
1.		
2.		
3.		
4.		
5.		

reduce the turnover of key R&D staff from 10 per cent to 5 per cent within a year. You could use surveys to find out some of the 'soft' issues, such as whether staff feel that team working has improved. Do make sure that each objective has at least one measure and pass mark assigned to it. What is the point of an objective if you do not know whether you have achieved it?

UNDERPINNING PHILOSOPHIES

The big question to answer is how important is pay in motivating staff? In some industries and occupations it is way ahead of everything else; in other organizations, non-pay issues can also be important to staff. Organizations that invest in training and development are often good at recruiting and retaining staff. Some jobs can be intrinsically satisfying. The caring professions have often attracted people with a strong sense of vocation who have rejected more highly paid careers. High status professions can retain staff at lower rates of pay than they might receive elsewhere, as has often been true of academia.

Flexible working hours and part-time employment can be very attractive to staff with family responsibilities. Some employers offer extensive social welfare packages including sports facilities, crèche facilities, health screening and private health insurance.

Some firms seek to increase employee commitment by encouraging share ownership or paying staff a percentage of the profits. You need to think carefully about the percentage variable pay that would be acceptable to your less well-off staff. Their building society and supermarket managers unfortunately do not show the same flexibility when they are asked to accept reduced payments.

Other firms give staff security through a no compulsory redundancy policy. Such a policy may be difficult to honour. Alternatively, an employer could reduce pay as in the case study opposite.

Many employers feel unable to provide guaranteed employment. Instead some are offering their staff employability: they will train and develop their staff to a high standard, so if they are made redundant they can find another job much more easily.

The importance staff attach to pay as against other employment benefits varies between organizations and types of staff. Therefore, you should find out the views of your own staff and tailor their reward strategy accordingly.

The next few pages review the various approaches to reward. We will describe these to you and help you decide which is the most suitable for your organization.

JOB EVALUATION

Job evaluation is a means of paying the 'rate for the job' by systematically assessing jobs against agreed criteria. This approach was particularly popular in large, complex organizations in the 1970s and 1980s. Staff may well consider it fairer than other approaches as it has a greater element of consistency. Job evaluation is most effective where internal pay relativities are not threatened by a very competitive labour market. It also requires a stable organizational structure. The actual process of evaluating jobs can be speeded up by using PC-based programs. Job evaluation is less suited to dynamic organizations, where change is a constant feature. It is also less relevant to flatter structures with fewer job types. In addition, it can encourage an 'it's not in my job description' mentality. Job evaluation can also encourage staff to seek extra pay for each new activity they undertake by asking for their jobs to be re-evaluated.

Case study: Sharing the pain – Nucor Steel, USA

> Nucor Steel has a very high level of productivity and in 1992 the average output per employee was 1200 tons compared with an industry average of 450 tons. Its average rate of pay is much more than the industry average. Employee turnover is less than 1 per cent.
>
> The company has a no redundancy agreement. During a recession the pay of hourly paid workers and foreman is cut by 20–25 per cent. The pay of department heads is reduced to a greater extent – as much as 35–40 per cent – because a significant element of their pay is based on profits. The pay of the very top management drops more drastically by 65–70 per cent. In one recession the pay of the CEO fell from $460,000 to $108,000.
>
> *Source:* F. Kenneth Iverson (1993), 'Changing the Rules of the Game', *Planning Review*, September/October

TYPES OF REWARD STRATEGY

COMPETENCY-BASED PAY

Competency-based pay rewards staff for the number, depth and types of their skills that are deemed to be of value to the company. This system encourages employee flexibility and learning. It is increasingly popular in 'learning organizations' or in organizations with many knowledge workers. Fewer managers are needed if staff acquire more vertical skills, and it also supports more participative management. The skills acquired, however, must add value to the organization. They also need to be used often enough for staff to retain their competence and efficiency. This reward strategy is probably better suited to staff lower down the organization, than senior staff. Additionally, learning organizations need to afford the big investment in training. A disadvantage is that the employer may lose control of the pay bill.

GAINSHARING

Gainsharing seeks to improve productivity by paying some of the resulting savings as bonuses to staff, often on a 50:50 basis. Gainsharing requires good information systems that can accurately measure changes in output and cost. It may also be used to support TQM by rewarding lower defect rates. The attraction of gainsharing is that it is easy to understand, it is self-financing and can be used to reward team effort. It is more attractive to poor performing organizations that have plenty of leeway to make up. However, gainsharing is difficult to sustain after a few years, by when most of the big improvements in efficiency have been realized. Another problem is that gainsharing can be divisive where units are assessed individually and some units are much more efficient than others. The least efficient units would have the largest scope for gainsharing, which rewards

Case study: Gainsharing – Evart Products, USA

Evart is a car component supplier that had a bad reputation for quality. After introducing gainsharing, its defect rate went down from 437 to 2 per 10000. The company see the main benefit as better quality, rather than lower costs, although it is not clear whether they calculated the true cost of defects in terms of reworking and wasted materials. Had the company introduced a full-fledged TQM programme, this would have been established, as we saw in Chapter 5.

Gainsharing was linked to a structured employee suggestion scheme. The 1000 employees were grouped into 23 teams that met at least once a month to make suggestions. They covered ways to cut costs, reduce waste and streamline procedures. Staff made 4329 suggestions over a four-year period. Ideas costing under $200 affecting only the working area of a particular team could be implemented immediately. Over 80 per cent of suggestions fell into this category. More costly and ambitious suggestions were referred to three senior review teams of representatives of area teams and management. At the top of the hierarchy, the board reviewed suggestions and monitored performance against plans. This is very much the TQM quality circle model.

The main lessons learnt were as follows:

O   Leadership from the chief executive was essential.
O   The benefits were long term.
O   Involve employees fully from the outset.
O   Allow employees time off work.
O   Supply employees regularly with information on organizational performance.
O   Train supervisors and managers to become facilitators.

The main outcomes were as follows:

O   Better quality.
O   Some reduction in costs.
O   Improved sales and more secure employment.
O   Better communication and employee involvement.
O   Improved self-management by staff.

The staff were pleased with their bonuses in the first two years of the scheme. However, its popularity fell when there were no payments in the third year, due to a fall in sales during a recession.

Source: Timothy Ross and Larry Hatcher (1992), 'Gainsharing Drives Quality Improvement', *Personnel Journal,* November.

previous poor management. Staff in the most efficient units could claim that they have already achieved savings before gainsharing, for which they have not been compensated. High performing individuals in a poor-performing company will not receive the reward they feel they deserve.

PERFORMANCE APPRAISAL

Many organizations have adopted performance appraisal in response to growing competitive pressures. If you select this approach you must communicate your strategic direction, goals and results regularly and in a way that all your staff can understand. Performance appraisal assumes that you can identify an individual or team's contribution to performance. Can you do that for all your staff? Performance measures can be 'soft' ones that are difficult to measure, 'hard' ones that are easy to quantify, or a combination of both. 'Hard' performance measures include the following:

O   Sales.
O   Output.
O   Profits.
O   Share values.
O   Customer attitudes measured by independently administered surveys.

When setting performance standards for 'hard' measures it is important at the outset to consider how the positive/negative impact of forces beyond the immediate control of scheme participants will be dealt with when evaluating overall performance at the year end. What if you had a freak event such as a hurricane that doubled the sale of your chainsaws? There are also problems about who is responsible for success within the organization. Higher sales may be due to a better performance from your sales staff. Alternatively, they may be due to the introduction of a very well-designed new product. In which case the designers may argue that the sales bonuses really belong to them! In some cases sudden increases in sales can be counterproductive. They can be generated by sales staff offering discounts to boost their performance figures just before a periodic review. This would be particularly costly where expensive overtime had to be worked to fulfil the orders. It would be even more expensive still if it resulted in disgruntled customers having to wait longer for their deliveries. Another difficult question is how to reward improved output due to increased automation that may have made the task of production workers easier. To what extent should operative staff be rewarded for such a change?

Some schemes seek the best of all worlds. They combine financial, operational and customer-based approaches. For instance, profits over a certain amount can be distributed to staff if certain production, quality and customer targets are met.

The most common form of appraisal is conducted by superiors of their subordinates. This is most suited to a hierarchical organization where the boss is able to assess all aspects of the subordinate's contribution. It is less useful in a delayered organization where the superior may not be sufficiently knowledgeable because of the wide span of control. It is also problematic in a matrix organization where an individual could have several bosses.

Appraisal by peers and subordinates (upward appraisal) is most suited to situations where these staff have more contact with the appraisee than the boss, as in many delayered organizations. Upward appraisal is usually conducted anonymously. Anonymity is best maintained when five or more subordinates are involved. The appraisal needs to be handled sensitively so that managers do not see it as a threat. One way to reduce this possibility is to ask the appraisee to nominate a number of peers and subordinates to carry out the appraisal. This type of appraisal may well suit an organization that places a high priority on empowering its staff.

Appraisal by external and internal customers has been introduced by organizations seeking to become more extrovert and get closer to the customer. It avoids the nightmare scenario of high bonuses being paid based on internal judgements when sales may actually be falling due to customer dissatisfaction!

There is a growing range of appraisal systems to meet the needs of very different organizations. The inputs could be made by a variety of people:

O   Superiors.
O   Peers.
O   Subordinates.
O   Internal customers.
O   External customers.

Several types of appraisal can be used together to reflect different aspects of performance. This approach is particularly important if you are going to delayer your organization. Managers will have more people directly reporting to them and will have less opportunity to see them in action.

INDIVIDUAL PERFORMANCE-RELATED PAY

Originally, individual performance-related pay (IPRP) was used for top managers. Over the last decade, there has been a growth in such schemes and their coverage has been extended down the organization. Managers usually agree objectives after discussing them with the postholder. Often this approach involves some objectives being passed down the organization with little scope to modify them.

Typically, the manager meets the member of staff to review his or her performance against the targets. The performance of a subordinate is usually reviewed on a regular basis, usually annually. Some organizations have fixed criteria, while others leave it to the main players to decide them.

An important part of performance appraisal is goal-setting. Goal-setting involves the manager and the subordinate, and its main features should be as follows:

O   **Clear** goals state what should be achieved and when.

O   **Challenging** goals should stretch staff.
O   **Commitment** to goals must be obtained through discussion.
O   **Comment** on performance should be given.

Organizations need to decide on the percentage of pay that should be performance-related. The amount needs to be large enough to make an impact.

❖   **Health warning +**

There is a serious danger of IPRP becoming discredited as a 'form-filling exercise', if managers do not treat it as a high priority and devote enough time to it.

The usual objectives of IPRP can be an uneasy amalgam of deciding on merit pay and career progression, or lack of it on the one hand and on individual development needs on the other. It is a brave or foolhardy soul who volunteers development needs that might encourage an employer to score them down on pay!
    Performance-related pay is based on the following assumptions:

O   Most aspects of performance can be measured.
O   Each individual's contribution can be separately identified.
O   Managers have the skill and confidence to measure performance.
O   Managers see enough of their staff to know how they perform.
O   Managers mark consistently.
O   Staff will work harder if they are paid more.
O   Staff who fail to meet the standard will try harder.

Separating out an individual's contribution can be much harder than it might seem. For instance how much are they dependent on the support and cooperation of others? Staff would feel aggrieved if their performance suffered due to the bloodymindness of colleagues. However, how happy would you be in rewarding staff who happened to have very helpful co-workers?
    It can be difficult for a scheme to be seen as fair by all staff. There are some instances of appraisals discriminating against women and ethnic minorities and organizations need to monitor schemes carefully to ensure that such discrimination does not take place.
    There is a great deal of debate about the value of performance-related pay. Deming was very opposed and wrote:

> It leaves people bitter, crushed, bruised, battered, desolate, despondent, dejected, feeling inferior, some even depressed, unfit for work for weeks after receipt of rating, unable to comprehend why they are inferior. It is unfair, as it ascribes to the people in a group differences that may be caused totally by the system they work in.

(Deming, 1986)

Many organizations limit the number of staff who can be assigned to the higher achievement bands, thus keeping performance pay within a given budget. The way staff see this is that no matter how hard they work, they may still fall just outside the better reward categories. It also means that there are a predetermined number of people who are scored as failures. For many schemes the majority of staff are given an average rating. How good is that for their morale? Would you work harder if you were told that your performance was average for several years in succession? Telling staff that their performance is in the bottom category or merely average may demotivate them. It also encourages employees to compete against each other, rather than work for the good of the organization as Deming pointed out in an interview in the *Wall Street Journal* (4 June 1990).

LINKING REWARD STRATEGIES TO ORGANIZATIONAL CHANGE

Having reviewed the strengths and weaknesses of the different approaches to reward, you are now in a position to select the one most suited to your organizational culture. You also need to link reward to your strategy for organizational change as we have done below.

EMPOWERMENT AND PARTICIPATIVE APPROACHES TO REWARD

You can increase staff commitment to your reward strategy by involving them in its design and implementation. Set up work groups representing the different levels and parts of your organization and coordinate their work carefully. James Goodale (1992) sets out the main steps for the group working to design an appraisal system as follows:

1.   Identify goals and the problems to avoid.
2.   Define the types of performance using directly observable, job-related behaviour, avoiding subjective assessment of personality.
3.   Design policies and procedures.

If encouraging your staff to suggest improvements is an important part of your empowerment programme, you could consider what financial rewards might be attractive to them.

TQM AND REWARD STRATEGY

Competency-based pay is consistent with TQM as staff are rewarded for skills that make a significant contribution to quality. You can use gainsharing to reward staff for reducing error rates and wastage.

We have heard the strong arguments against individually based performance pay and TQM. Implicit in performance appraisal is the notion that low productivity is caused by individuals and groups not working hard enough. This attitude tends to ignore the impact of systems on productivity. It may be that much larger gains in productivity and quality can be achieved by staff working differently using new systems rather than working harder using old ones. Carson, Cardy and Dobbins (1992) argue that 'total quality management proponents argue that performance appraisal is an attempt by management to pin the blame of poor organizational performance on lower level employees, rather than focusing attention on the system, for which upper management is primarily responsible.' This argument is precisely the one used to justify re-engineering, namely that poor processes are a key source of poor performance.

Reward systems consistent with TQM tend to reduce differences between individuals. Carson, Cardy and Dobbins suggest that it is possible to reconcile TQM and performance management by following these steps:

1.   Train appraisers to identify faults in organizational systems and how they may affect performance.
2.   Multiple types of assessors – self-assessment by staff should be linked to appraisal by their managers; this could be extended to include peer review.
3.   Appraisal interviews should concentrate on how to remove barriers to improvement.
4.   Minimize differentiation between employees. It is argued that most employees should be categorized as 'good'.
5.   Team-based evaluation should be considered and this may even be used with individual appraisal.
6.   Performance measures should be designed to cover a wide range of objective and subjective measures.

As with empowerment, you need to think about rewarding staff for their suggestions. Some will argue that if you have established a culture of continuous improvement such payments are unnecessary as it is seen to be a part of everyone's job. But staff may feel aggrieved if their ideas save their organization huge amounts of money and none of it is shared with them.

RE-ENGINEERING AND REWARD STRATEGY

When processes have been redesigned it is essential to reward all those involved in a particular process consistently. This will tend to rule out IPRP and favour competency-based pay or gainsharing.

PICK AND MIX

If none of the above approaches is in tune with your own approach to organizational change, you might be attracted to a hybrid, pick and mix action plan suggested by Judith Bardwick in her book *Danger in the Comfort Zone* (1991). Her research shows that executives need to convert their workforces from the psychology of entitlement to the psychology of earning. Once elevated from the security of entitlement (with its assured salary increases, bonuses and promotions) to a culture of earning, many organizations have found that employees will become more creative, confident and productive.

The main steps Bardwick identifies for this psychological move are as follows:

1.   Identify and evaluate real work. Start by reviewing all jobs objectively and systematically and agree a process for evaluating real performance.

Opportunities should be created for challenge and risk-taking by releasing people for special assignments and job rotation. Each year 25 per cent of a person's job should be new.

2. Increase visibility and peer pressure. Assign work to small groups of people of similar status whenever possible. Evaluate groups instead of individual performance as this encourages peer pressure, group-bonding and emotional support. Nissan, which uses no time clocks, boasts the best attendance record in the USA. It achieves this as its teams have fewer than 20 members, so absentees are noticed. Japanese car makers do not use relief workers to cover for absentees so team members must provide this cover themselves.

3. Consider incentive pay plans. General Motors Saturn Division set salaries at 80 per cent of the union scale. Workers earned the difference by reaching productivity targets and undergoing training.

4. Fire non-performers. Convince people that underachievers who receive ample evaluation, guidance and support to help them perform at an acceptable level are sacked if they continue to underachieve.

5. Create competition – either against external competitors or by getting people to compete against their earlier achievements but *not* with each other.

6. Create a meritocracy, where people at all levels can earn the right to participate, influence, decide and lead. Skill level not status counts the most.

❖ **Health warning +**

Where an organization is operating in a matrix framework, i.e. people have functional and process responsibilities, ensure that the reward strategy gives priority to the process rather than the functional element.

SELECTING YOUR REWARD STRATEGY BASED ON YOUR APPROACH TO ORGANIZATIONAL CHANGE

Table 11.3 relates some organizational strategies to the reward options.

Now rate your future strategy against the success factors listed in Table 11.4. How did you get on? Answers rated 'weak' or 'very weak' suggest that you need to review your strategy. You really ought to aim at a score of at least 14. If not, start again.

TABLE 11.3   LINKING REWARD TO ORGANIZATIONAL STRATEGY

Organizational strategy	Reward option
Delayering	Reward growth in job – less promotion possible. Where appraisal is used, the increase in direct reports means that managers should take into account the views of customers, peers and subordinates on their staff.
Empowerment	Participative approaches to designing your reward strategy.
TQM	Flat rate of pay, or pay based on quality, competencies, or gainsharing.
Business process re-engineering	Reward based on a whole process.
Learning organization	Competency-based pay – pay for knowledge.
Stable environment, large number of different jobs	Pay based on job evaluation.

TABLE 11.4   SUCCESS FACTORS OF A REWARD STRATEGY

Success factor	Very strong 5	Strong 4	Somewhat weak 3	Weak 2	Very weak 1
Attractive to the right calibre of staff					
Easily understood by staff					
Felt fair by staff					
Affordable beyond the short term					
Total					

CHECKLIST FOR MANAGEMENT ACTION

1.   Define the objectives of your reward strategy using Table 11.1 and ensure that they are consistent with your strategy for organizational change.
2.   Formulate your success criteria using Table 11.2.
3.   Establish what your staff want from a reward package. Either involve them directly in its design or carry out a staff survey.
4.   Relate reward strategy to employee preferences and organizational objectives.
5.   What needs to be done to support the new strategy, e.g. training and involving staff in design?
6.   Implement your reward strategy.
7.   Monitor the results.

AFTERWORD

We won't grow unless we take risks. Any successful
company is riddled with failures.
James E. Burke, chairman, Johnson and Johnson

Now that you have completed your first voyage of discovery you are ready
to go out and sail the seas of change for real. You will be confident of
how ready your ship and crew are for the journey ahead. You will have
a fairly clear idea of the final destination and how you will get there. Here are a
few final tips before you set sail.

Always have a clear view of the outcomes of each main step on the way to
change. For instance, how will you know that you have actually achieved it?
How will other people such as staff and customers know this too? Make sure that
each step is a small one. That way you will soon know whether you are going
in the right direction. It will also be good for everyone's morale to obtain
feedback and some quick wins, even small ones.

Our own experience teaches us that it is easy to underestimate the resources
necessary to achieve change. The military have a theory of overwhelming force
where for an offensive to succeed they use three attackers for every defender.
When it comes to estimating the extent of your overwhelming resource, take into
account how many champions you have. In addition find out how well
entrenched and powerful are the opponents of change. The number of waverers
must be identified. Also take account of your organization's previous experience
of change. The more painful the events, the more resource you will need to
compensate.

If the ideas that you are going to implement fit in with your organization's
culture and the predilection of your CEO, then you are likely to succeed and get
promoted into the bargain! Alternatively, if you feel that you need to challenge
some of the prevailing ideas of change then you will need a few tricks up your
sleeve. Ensure that you are aware of the agenda of your key bosses. What do they
want to achieve? What are their fears? How can your preferred approach to change
be sold to them in their language? Could the use of case studies influence your
more practically minded bosses? Is there some robust evidence of external threads
to your organization that could make it easier for them to take difficult decisions?

If your organization is accustomed to a top-down style of management, it will have to make large changes to become more in tune with our times. The organizations of today and tomorrow will need highly committed, well-educated and trained staff, the latest technology, and efficient and effective ways of working. We all need to become more comfortable with taking calculated risks. We need to plant many ideas and approaches as only a few are likely to blossom. We should be modest enough to realize that we cannot know which ones will flourish in our increasingly unpredictable environment.

REFERENCES

Anderson Consulting (1993) *Patient Centred Care*, London: Anderson Consulting.

Arkin, Anat (1995), 'Self-renewing Companies', *People Management*, 19 October, p. 37.

Bardwick, Judith (1991), *Danger in the Comfort Zone*, New York: AMACOM Books.

Belasco, James A. (1990), *Teaching the Elephant to Dance*, London: Century Business.

Bernbach, William, quoted in Julia Vitullo-Martin and Robert J. Moskin (1994), New York: Oxford University Press, p. 122.

Bott, Keith and Johnson, Ron (1992), 'New Strands for Quality', *Personnel Management*, July, pp. 36–9.

Bowen and Lawler (1992), *Sloan Management Review*, Spring (from MIT) Reprint 3323.

British Quality Foundation (1994), *The 1995 UK Quality Award*, London: British Quality Foundation, p. 9.

Calloway, Wayne (1991), *Fortune*, 11 March.

Carson, Kenneth, Cardy, Robert and Dobbins, Gregory (1992), 'Upgrade the Employee Evaluation Process', *HR Magazine*, November, p. 88.

Caudron, Sari (1993), 'Keys to Starting a TQM Programme', *Personnel Journal*, February.

Chen, Eva (1993), 'Total Quality Management in a Small, High Technology Company', *California Management Review*, Spring.

Connock, Stephen (1991), *HR Vision*, London: IPM.

Deming, W. E. (1986), *Out of the Crisis: Quality, Productivity and Competitive Position*, MIT Centre for Advanced Engineering Study, Cambridge, MA: Cambridge University Press.

Department of Trade and Industry (1993), *Competitiveness of the UK Manufacturing Industry*, Evidence to the House of Commons, 14 July London: HMSO.

The Economist (1992), 22 February p. 82.

The Economist (1992), 4 April pp. 15, 20.

The Economist (1995), 2 September p. 83.

The Financial Times (1993), 10 February p. 14.

The Financial Times (1994), 26 July.

Geber, Beverley (1992), 'Saturn Grand Experiment', *Training Magazine*, June.

Golzen, Godfrey (1992), 'Giving Power to the People', *The Sunday Times*, 15 November.

Goodale, James (1992), 'Improving Performance Appraisal', *Business Quarterly*, Autumn, pp. 65–70.

The Guardian (1995), 6 September, p. 3.

Hammer, Michael (1990), 'Re-engineer Work – Don't Automate, Obliterate', *Harvard Business Review*, July–August.

Hammer, Michael and Champy, James (1993), *Re-engineering the Corporation*, London: Nicholas Brearley, p. 32.

Handy, Charles (1991), *Age of Unreason*, London: Business Books, p. 72.

Harper, Bob and Harper, Ann (1989), *Succeeding as a Self Directed Work Team*, New York: MW Corporation.

Harvey-Jones, John (1988), *Making it Happen*, Glasgow: William Collins.

Hinterbuber, Hans H. and Levin, Boris M. (1994), *Strategic Networks – The organization of the future*, Long Range Planning, Vol. 27, (3), p. 46.

Hofer, C. and Schedel, D. (1978), Boston Consulting Group Matrix, *Strategic Formulation: Analytical Concepts*, West Publishing Co.

Iverson, F. Kenneth (1993), 'Changing the Rules of the Game', *Planning Review*, September/October.

Jay, Ros (1995), *Build a Great Team*, London: Pitman.

Johansson, Henry, McHugh, Patrick, Pendlebury, John and Wheeler, William (1993), *Business Process Re-engineering: Breakpoint Strategies for Market Dominance*, Chichester: John Wiley & Sons.

Johnson, Gerry and Scholes, Kevan (1988), *Exploring Corporate Strategy*, second edition, London: Prentice Hall.

Kano, Noriaki, Seraku, Nobuhijo and Tsuji, Shinichi (1991), *Attractive Quality and Must be Quality*, Methuen, MA: GOAL/QPC.

Kanter, Rosabeth Moss (1992), *When Giants Learn To Dance*, London: Routledge & Kegan Paul.

Lawler III, Edward (1992), *Employee Involvement and Total Quality Management*, California: Jossey Bass.

Lawton, Robin (1992), 'Applying Customer-centred Quality to Human Resource', *National Productivity Review*, Summer.

Levitt, Ted (1990), *Thinking About Management*, London: Macmillan.

Lewin, Kurt (1947), 'Frontiers in Group Dynamics: Concept, Method, and Reality in Social Science, *Human Relations*, Vol. 1, June, pp. 5–14.

Lewin, Kurt (1951), *Field Theory in Social Sciences*, New York: Harper and Row.

Mahen, Tampoe (1994), '*Exploiting the Core Competencies of Your Organisation*', Long Range Planning, Vol. 27, August, pp. 68 and 69.

Marshall, Ray and Tueber, Marie (1992), *Thinking for a Living*, New York: Basic Books.

Meyer, Arnoud de, quoted by S. Lawrence in (1993) 'Quality has failed to lead to profitability', *Personnel Management*, August, p. 14.

Milkovich, George and Milkovich, Carolyn (1992), 'Strengthening the Pay-performance Relationship: The Research', *Compensation & Benefits Review*, November–December, p. 54.

Mills, D. Quinn (1992), *Rebirth of the Corporation*, New York: John Wiley.

Nadler, David (1992), *Fortune*, 19 May.

Ohmae, Kenichi (1982), *The Mind of the Strategist*, Harmondsworth: Penguin Books, p. 26.

Oram, M. and Wellin, R. (1995), *Re-engineering's Missing Ingredient: The Human Factor*, London: IPD.

Osstreff, Frank and Smith, D. (1992), 'The Search for the Organization of Tomorrow,' *Fortune*, 18 May.

Pedler, Mike, Burgoyne, John and Boydell, Tom (1991), *The Learning Company*, Maidenhead: McGraw Hill.

Peters, Tom (1984) *Thriving on Chaos*, London: Pan.

Redmand, Tom and Snape, Ed (1992), 'Upward and onward; can staff appraise their manager?', *Personnel Review*, 21 July, p. 32.

Ripley, Robert E. and Ripley, Marie J. (1992), 'Empowerment, the Cornerstone of Quality: Empowering Management in Innovative Organisations in the 1990s', *Management Decision*, Vol. 30, No. 4, pp. 20–43.

Ross, Timothy and Hatcher, Larry (1992), 'Gainsharing Drives Quality Improvement', *Personnel Journal*, November.

RSA (1994), *Tomorrow's Company: the Role of Business in a Changing World*, London: RSA.

Rubenowitz, Sigvard (1992), 'The Role of Management in Production Units with Autonomous Work Groups', *International Journal of Operations & Production Management*, Vol. 12, Nos. 7/8, pp. 103–16.

Scholtes, Peter (1993), 'Total Quality of Performance Appraisal: Choose One', *National Productivity Review*, Summer, p. 358.

Semler, Ricardo (1993), *MAVERICK!*, London: Century.

Sheridan, J.H. (1991), 'America's Best Plants: Tennessee Eastman', *Industry Week*, October, pp. 59–80.

Smart, Geoffrey (1995), 'Don't be a systems victim', *Internal Auditing*, December.

Smith, John *The Twenty-sixth International Hospital Congress* 'The Patient Focused Hospital' Booz Allen & Hamilton, (1989), The Hague, Netherlands, 31 May.

Sommerlatte, Tom (1994), quoted by Jan Stiles, 'Strategic Alliance: Making Them Work', *Long Range Planning*, Vol. 27, August, p. 134.

Stafford, Edwin R. (1994), 'Using co-operative Strategies to Make Alliances Work', *Long Range Planning*, Vol. 27, No. 3, p. 70.

Stewart, Thomas A. (1992), 'The Search for the Organisation of Tomorrow', Fortune, 18 May, pp. 67–72.

Talwar, Rohit (1993), 'Business Re-engineering – A Strategy Driven Approach', *Long Range Planning*, Vol. 26, No. 56, pp. 23, 36.

Tomasko, Robert (1992), 'Restructuring: Getting it Right', *Management Review*, April , pp. 10–15.

Towers, John (1992), 'A New Deal', *Manufacturing Engineering*, July.

UK Quality (1995), March, pp. 20–25.

Walker, Terry (1992), 'Creating Total Quality Improvement that Lasts', *National Productivity Review*, Autumn.

Waterman, Robert H. (1982), 'The Seven Elements of Strategic Fit', *Journal of Business Strategy*, Vol. 2, No 3 (Winter).

Watzlawick, Paul, Weakland John and Fisch, Richard (1974), *Change* New York: Norton.

Weatherly, Jonathan (1992), 'Dare to Compare for Better Productivity', *HR Magazine*, September.

Webb, Sue (1989), 'Blue Print for Success', *Industrial Society*, May.

Weisbord, Marvin (1992), *Discovering Common Ground: How Future Search Conferences are used to Achieve Breakthrough, Innovation, Empowerment, Shared Vision and Collaboraive Action*, Maidenhead: McGraw-Hill.

Wellins, R. and Rick, S. (1995), 'Taking Account of the Human Factor', *People Management*, 19 October, pp. 30–32.

Zemke, Ron (1993), 'A Guide to TQM', *Training*, April, pp. 48–52.

INDEX

DATE DUE

AUG 7 '04			

HIGHSMITH #45115